精神力補充手冊
Spiritual Forces Supplement

Author / 编著：Long Xuan（龍軒）

你是幸運的人，接下來的時間，你即將獲得一個
更真實、更優化的自己

The mystery you want to know is in it.
You are part of the Great Spirit and the Great Spirit
will always be with you

Title: Spiritual Forces Supplement
中文书名:《精神力补充手册》

Author / 编著: Long Xuan（龍軒）

English proofreading by Xiyang Pan（返本歸真）

ISBN: 978-1-967799-84-8

Publisher / 出版商:
Asian Culture Press LLC
1942 Broadway St., Suite 314c
Boulder, CO 80302
United States

Disclaimer

This book is intended for personal spiritual growth and self-reflection only. It does not constitute medical, psychological, legal, or religious advice. The author and publisher assume no responsibility for any actions taken based on the content of this book.

Concepts such as "spirit," "soul," "spirituality," and "karma" represent the author's personal perspectives and do not reflect the doctrines or positions of any religion or religious organization.

免责声明（中文）

本书内容仅供个人精神成长与自我反思之参考，不构成任何医疗、心理治疗、法律或宗教建议。作者及出版商不对读者基于本书内容所作出的任何个人决定或行为结果承担责任。

书中所涉及的"精神""灵魂""灵性""因果"等概念，均为作者个人理解与表达，不代表任何宗教立场、教义或组织观点。

First Paperback Edition, 2026
Printed in the United States of America

能爲龍軒的新書《精神力補充手冊》寫序，我感到非常榮幸。

It is my great honor to write the foreword for Long Xuan's new book, Spiritual Forces Supplement.

我與龍軒的相識，緣起於一本對我們人生觀產生深遠影響的書——《海奧華預言》。多年來，我與許多讀者探討過這本書，而在所有人之中，龍軒是理解最爲透徹的少數之一。也正因這份共鳴，我們成了非常要好的兄弟。他將自己對《海奧華預言》的理解和一些個人感悟，融合在一起，總結出了這本《精神力補充手冊》。

My acquaintance with Long Xuan began through a book that had a profound influence on our worldview — Thiaoouba Prophecy. Over the years, I have discussed this book with many readers, and among them, Long Xuan is one of the very few who truly grasp its essence. It was this shared understanding that brought us together as close brothers. In this work, he combines his deep insights into Thiaoouba Prophecy with his personal reflections, distilling them into Spiritual Forces Supplement.

我們都知道有關輪迴的本質——此生的物質身體只是我們靈體學習的載具，最重要的則是我們靈魂本身的提升與經歷。而這本《精神力補充手冊》將以一個淺顯易懂的方式，幫助我們的靈體

"充能"，當有緣人讀到這本書時，定能從此書中受益。

We all understand the essence of reincarnation — that our physical body in this life is merely a vehicle for our Astral body to learn and grow. What truly matters is the elevation and experience of our soul itself. This book offers a clear and accessible way to "recharge" the spirit, and those destined to encounter it will surely benefit from its wisdom.

我們都是 Great Spirit 的一部分，本就是一體，我與龍軒都願意以我們各自的方式，去分享這些知識，幫助更多人認識真正的自己，理解生命的意義。願你在閱讀的旅程中，收穫屬於你的能量與祝福。

We are all part of the Great Spirit, and in truth, we are one. Both Long Xuan and I are committed, in our own ways, to sharing this knowledge, helping more people discover their true selves and understand the meaning of life. May you, on this journey through its pages, receive the energy and blessings that are meant for you.

——熊與海奧華

—— Bear & Thiaoouba

前 言
Preface

　　隨著"科技時代"的不斷發展，人們對"物質生活"的追求也越來越高。但隨之出現的一個現象也很奇怪，就是現代人的生活雖然物質上豐富了，可多數人還是感覺不到真正的快樂和幸福，內心反而經常會感到空虛。

With the continuous development of the "science and technology era", people's pursuit of "material life" is getting higher and higher. However, there is also a strange phenomenon that although modern people's lives are materially rich, most people still can't feel genuine joy and happiness, but often feel empty inside.

　　其實出現這種現象的最主要原因就是：現在的大多數人，只顧著在物質上豐富自己，卻忽略了自己在精神方面的正確培養。

In fact, the main reason for this phenomenon is that most people nowadays only focus on enriching themselves materially, but neglected the correct cultivation of their spirituality.

　　由於現代的人們每天通過手機、平板等電子產品，接收的信息量太大太多，多數人已經很難再去耐心讀完一本長篇書籍。所以，編輯了一本手冊跟大家分享 [1]，每篇文章的文字都很短，內容也沒有溢美之詞，簡潔易懂。

Due to the fact that humans on Earth receive an enormous amount of information every day through electronic products such as mobile phones and tablets, it is difficult for most people to read a long book patiently. Therefore, I have compiled a handbook to share with you [1]. The text of each article is very short, and the content is not overly embellished, so it is simple and easy to understand.

細心的讀者在認真閱讀三遍之後，會在心智和精神層面上獲得提升。

Careful readers will be improved mentally and spiritually after reading it three times carefully.

當然，如果有讀者願意按照手冊上的"指引"去改變自己，並堅持一段時間，那麼你一定會獲得一個更優化、更真實的自己。

Of course, if any reader is willing to change himself according to the "guidance" in the handbook and persist for a period of time, then you will definitely get a more optimized and more genuine self.

短文之間沒有刻意追求連貫性。儘管文中使用了部分"宗教性用詞"，但編寫者和文中的內容不代表任何宗教立場。

There is no deliberate pursuit of coherence among the short articles. Although some "religious terms" are used in the text, the author and the content of the text have nothing to do with any religion.

龍軒

Long Xuan

2022 年 10 月

October 2022

注 Note

[1] 其中的某些文章我不確定是怎麼想出來的（尤其是後邊的那些文章），因為在某些時候，我的腦子裡會突然冒出一段文字，我需要馬上編寫出來發給自己。比如有時我正在開車，腦海中的文字出現了，我需要立刻把車停到路邊，然後編輯這一段話發給自己。有時是在睡醒之後，有時在睡覺之前，也有時在靜心冥想之後……就這樣一段段文字，拼接形成了一篇篇短文。

我感覺這些短文應該讓更多的人知道，也許是我的"高我"想借用我的手，把這些文字寫出來，傳遞給大家，希望對大家有所幫助。

如果你能耐心地閱讀幾遍這些短文和短文中多次提到的那本書，那麼你的內心一定會獲得前所未有的平靜和一種脫胎換骨的自由。

For some of these articles, I'm not sure how I came up with them (especially the later ones), because at some point, a piece of text would suddenly pop up in my mind and I need to write it down and send it to myself immediately. For instance, sometimes when I'm driving and words pop up in my mind, I need to pull over to the side of the road immediately and then edit this passage to send to myself. Sometimes it is after waking up, sometimes before going to sleep, and sometimes after quiet meditation... just like this, paragraphs of text were pieced together to form short articles one after another.

I feel that these short articles should be known by more people. Perhaps it is my 'higher self' that wants to use my hands to write them down and share them with others, in the hope that they may be of help If you can patiently read these short essays several times, as well as the book that is repeatedly mentioned in them, you will surely gain an unprecedented sense of inner peace and a kind of transformative freedom.

目　錄
Catalogue

精神層面提升進化(中級)第17篇～第32篇
Spiritual Level Ascension Evolution (Intermediate) Articles 17 ~ 32

精神層面提升進化(高級)第33篇～第50篇
Spiritual Level Ascension Evolution (Advanced) Articles 33 ~ 50

精神層面提升進化 初級

Spiritual Level Ascension Evolution (Primary)

1

人只有保持身體的輕便，才能使靈性得到有效地提升
Only by keeping the body light can people improve their spirituality effectively.

如果一個人經常飲食過量，讓自己的胃超載，身體的精力就會過多地浪費在處理食物上。

If a person often overeats and overloads the stomach, the body wastes too much energy digesting food.

隨著一個人的體重不斷地增加，這個人就會被過重的身體所拖累，反應能力和大腦的思考力就會減弱。

As a person's weight keeps increasing, this person will be burdened by an overweight body, so their reaction ability and brain thinking ability will be weakened.

然而又因為此人過重的身體需要更多的熱量來運作，機體就會自動增加此人的飲食量，來達到運轉的目的。

However, because this person's overweight body requires more calories to function, the body will automatically increase this person's food intake to achieve the purpose of body operation.

這就是一個人"越愛吃越變胖，越變胖越愛吃"的原因，由此進入了一個可怕的循環。

This is the reason that "the more a person loves to eat, the fatter he gets, and the fatter he gets, the more he loves to eat", thus entering a terrible cycle.

所以，在這個"物質過剩，充滿誘惑"的時代裡，人們更應該多考慮自己的心神，應該控制自己的食欲和食量，讓身體的負擔變輕，才能有效地鍛煉靈性。

Therefore, in this era of "material surplus and temptation", people should pay more attention to their own minds, control their appetite and food intake, and lighten the burden on their bodies in order to effectively exercise spirituality.

隨著你的身體重回輕便，精神力也會得到恢復，在處理未來的事情上會更加高效敏捷。

As your body returns to lightness, your spiritual energy will be restored and you will be more efficient and agile in dealing with future things.

2

適當地控制重口味食物，可以使一個人在心智上得到提升
Proper control of extreme taste food
can improve one's mind

人體是一個非常精密的“處理系統”，任何食物，在進入人體之後都要進行運化和處理。但如果一個人長期飲食“口味過重”，那麼身體在處理這些食物時，就會“調用”更多的“精力”去完成運化和過濾。

The human body is a very sophisticated "processing system", and any food must be transported and processed after entering the human body. However, if a person's long-term diet "tastes too extreme", then the body will "call" more energy to complete the transportation and filtration when processing these foods.

比如，某些過甜、過鹹、過辣或過油膩的食品，這些“重口味”食品在被身體處理和過濾時，就會比處理和過濾“正常口味”的食品消耗更多的精神力。

For example, some foods are too sweet, too salty, too spicy or too greasy. These "extreme taste" foods will consume more spiritual energy when being processed and filtered by the body than those with "normal taste".

然而一個人每天的"精神力"是有限的，如果身體把過多的"精神力"用在了處理食物上，那麼身體就沒有足夠的"精神力"支配在這個人的大腦和心智上。

However, a person's daily "Spiritual energy" is limited. If the body spends too much "Spiritual energy" on handling food, then the body will not have enough "Spiritual energy" for the brain and mind.

我們要充分瞭解大自然為我們創造的身體，作為一名人類提升心智，發展靈性才是我們首要該做的事情，而不應是提升體重，滿足食欲。

We should fully understand the bodies that nature has created for us. As a human being, improving our minds and developing our spirituality should be our top priority, rather than merely increasing our weight or satisfying our appetite.

所以一個人如果想在改善心智、優化情緒、思維敏捷這些方面上提升自己，適當地控制"食量和重口味食物"這將是個有效的做法。

So if a person wants to improve themselves in terms of enhancing their mind, optimizing their mood and having quick thinking, appropriately controlling "food intake and extreme taste food" will be an effective approach.

3

人只有保持在"中間"平穩的情緒，才能使"能力"維持在最佳的位置

Only by maintaining a stable mood in the "middle" can people maintain their "ability" in the best position

一個人的情緒如果經常不穩定，那麼這個人的精神力就會被情緒所消耗。

If a person's mood is often unstable, then this person's spiritual energy will be consumed by emotions.

如果把人體比作成一個非常精密的"處理系統"，那麼"精神力"就是為人體系統提供能源的"電池"。

If the human body is compared to a very sophisticated "processing system", then "spiritual energy" is the "power source" that provides energy for the human body system.

舉個例子：一台計算機，如果在處理某些文檔或圖像時，機器的本身出現了過熱的"溫度"，那麼這台計算機的性能就會被產生的溫度所影響，從而導致機器的功耗變大，運轉變慢，直至出現死機等不良現象。

For example, if a computer has overheated "temperature" when processing some documents or images, the performance of the computer will be affected by the generated temperature, which will lead to the increase of power consumption and slow operation of the machine until it crashes.

然而人類的"系統"也會有同樣的事情發生。如果一個人在遇到某些事情時，情緒經常"爆發"[1]或者"低落"，那麼大腦的處理能力就會降到平時的最低值，也因此往往會出現錯誤的判斷。

However, the same thing can happen to the human "system". If a person's mood often "explodes" [1] or "feels depressed" when encountering certain things, then the processing ability of the brain will drop to its usual minimum, and as a result, wrong judgments will often occur.

這就是為什麼，在一個人的不良情緒平穩後，才會感到當時的做法是錯誤的，而為此後悔。

This is why it is only after a person's negative emotions have calmed down that they realize what they did at that time was wrong and regret it.

由於不良的情緒會過多地消耗精神力，時間久了身體就會出現"供電不足"的現象，身體的各種問題就會隨之發生。

Because negative emotions consume too much spiritual energy, over time, the body will experience a phenomenon of "insufficient power supply", and various problems will follow.

所以任何過亢過悲、過熱過冷的情緒，都會影響一個人正常的"運行"。

Therefore, any emotion that is too high or too low, too hot or too cold, will affect a person's normal "operation".

人類只有保持在"中間"平穩的情緒，才能使能力維持在最佳的位置，精神力才不會被情緒所浪費。

Only by maintaining a "middle" stable mood can humans maintain their abilities in the best position, and their spiritual energy will not be wasted by emotions.

注 Note

[1] 發怒是最容易消耗精神力的行為，佛陀曾說過這樣一段話，大致是："嗔怒會給你帶來痛苦，爭執便會帶來嗔怒。嗔怒就像在掌心點火，我們總想把它扔給別人，可在此之前，火卻會先燒到我們自己。"

Getting angry is the easiest way to drain spiritual energy. The Buddha once said something like this: "Anger will bring you pain, and disputes will bring anger." Anger is like lighting a fire in the palm of our hand. We always want to throw it at others, but before that, the fire will first reach ourselves.

4

請儘量避免不必要的"信息共振"
Please try to avoid unnecessary "information resonance"

人在情緒低落時，總會喜歡聽一些憂傷的歌曲，看一些憂傷的電視劇，或找個憂傷的人傾訴，這是因為此人當下的靈體振動與這些信息暫時產生了共鳴，所以才會喜歡。

When people are depressed, they always like to listen to some sad songs, watch some sad TV series, or talk to someone who is sad. This is because this person's current spiritual vibration resonates with these information temporarily, so they like it.

然而這是一個錯誤的做法，越是接收那些信息，越會延長一個人精神力的恢復時間。

However, this is a wrong approach. The more one receives that information, the longer it will take for his spiritual energy to recover.

舉個例子：一個喝醉的人，總希望有人再給他一瓶酒，然而如果你滿足了他，他就會加重醉酒的程度，從而使他清醒過來會更加困難。

For example, a drunk person always wants someone to give him another bottle of wine. However, if you satisfy him, he will be more drunk, which will make it more difficult for him to wake up.

所以，在任何時候，如果情緒低落，請避免不必要的信息共振。

Therefore, at any time, if you feel depressed, please avoid unnecessary information resonance.

你要做的是及時更正自己的態度[1]，多聽些歡快的歌曲，多看喜劇電影，多跟正能量的人交流，多接觸大自然，只有這樣才能讓精神力儘快得到恢復，才能處理好你遇到的所有問題。

What you have to do is to correct your attitude[1] in time, listen to more cheerful songs, watch more comedy movies, communicate with people with positive energy and get in touch with nature. Only in this way can your spiritual energy be restored as soon as possible and all the problems you encounter can be handled well.

注 Note

[1] 不要陷在過去，也不要焦慮未來，立刻更正態度，做好當下的自己，一切都會有最好的安排。

Don't get stuck in the past, and don't worry about the future. Correct your attitude immediately, be yourself in the present, and everything will be arranged for the best.

5

如何優化自己的面容、體型，讓自己變得更 "年輕"？
How to optimize your face and figure to make
yourself look younger?

一個人的精神貧瘠，將會負向影響他的物理外觀。

A person's psychic poverty will negatively affect his physical appearance.

相應地，一個人的精神層次如果得到提升，那麼他的物理外觀也會跟著獲得相應的改善。在面容、體型、年輕程度上，將會出現非常有益的改變。

Correspondingly, if a person's spiritual level is improved, his physical appearance will also be improved accordingly. There will be very beneficial changes in face, body shape, and youthfulness.

這就是為什麼同樣的年齡，有人看著年輕，而有人會看著蒼老，你會發現這不只是對身體保養的問題。

This is why at the same age, some people look young while others look old. You will find that this is not just a matter of taking care of your body.

然而一個人內在的精神，才是影響一個人物理外觀的主要原因。

However, a person's inner spirit is the main factor that affects their physical appearance.

6

冥想是最佳的"自我優化方式"之一
Meditation is one of the best ways of self-optimization

適當地練習冥想，可以使一個人在精神層面上得到提升。

Proper practice of meditation can improve one's spiritual level.

"你不需要去一個特別的地方，因為一個人最宏偉而且最美好的殿堂是他自己的內心 [1]。"

"You don't need to go to a special place, for the greatest and most beautiful temple of man is inside himself. [1]"

你只需要在一個安靜整潔的地方，關掉手機，靜下心來 [2]，閉上雙眼，盤腿而坐，後背挺直，思想放空一切，心裡只想著呼吸，這時你的大腦會主動得到"冷卻"，自身就會優化和梳理身體的各個方面，普通人練習冥想，最初每天只需 5 ～ 15 分鐘就可以。

You just need to turn off your cell phone in a quiet and tidy place, calm down [2], close your eyes, sit cross-legged, keep your back straight, empty your mind and just focus only on your breathing. At this time, your brain will take the initiative to "cool down" and your body will automatically optimize and sort out all aspects of your body. Ordinary people only need practice meditation for only 5 ~ 15 minutes a day at the beginning.

堅持練習冥想會獲得以下好處：梳理情緒，補充精神力，提高專注力，優化物理身體，增強記憶力，等等。

Practicing meditation regularly will bring you the following benefits: sorting out your emotions, replenishing your spiritual energy, improving your concentration, optimizing your physical body, enhancing your memory, and so on.

我們要充分瞭解大自然為我們創造的身體，也許"盤腿而坐，靜心冥想"的方式，早已是為"人類設定好"的優化方式。

We should fully understand the body that nature has created for us. Perhaps the way of "sitting cross-legged and meditating" has long been an optimized method "set for humans."

古代的那些智者和現代很多成功人士，都有冥想的習慣。所以，適當利用"冥想"去提升自己，將是個有效的做法。

The wise men in ancient times and many successful people in modern times have the habit of meditation. Therefore, it would be an effective way to use "meditation" appropriately to improve yourself.

注 Note

[1]"如果你想提升你自己，你必須冥想，然後專注；這兩者常常被混淆，但卻是不同的。你不需要去一個特別的地方，因為一個人

最宏偉而且最美好的殿堂是他自己的內心。"此段文字出自《海奧華預言》第十一章。（冥想和專注有所不同，冥想是放空，你可以只想著呼吸，盡量讓大腦思維變為一片空白。專注是集中，你可以把注意力集中到身體的某個部位，或眉心的位置）

"First if you want to 'elevate' yourself, you must meditate and then concentrate, which is different, although often the two are confused. You do not need to go to a special place, for the greatest and most beautiful temple of man is inside himself."This passage is from chapter 11 of "Thiaoouba prophecy". (Note: Meditation is different from concentration. Meditation is about emptying your mind. You can just think about breathing and try to make your brain blank. Concentration means focusing. You can focus your attention on a certain part of your body or the chakra between your eyebrows.)

這裡還要分享一個練習專注的方法："把你的大腦從所有的物質工作中解脫出來，要做到這一點，你需要後背靠著或是躺著，總之要讓你全身的肌肉放鬆。這樣可以減少你的大腦對你的各個身體部位的關注。遮住或閉上你的眼睛，這樣就不會有任何物體引起你的注意了——這是另一種放鬆大腦的方式。不要吃得太多或太少，兩者都不好。如果你吃得太多，你的胃就會超負荷，反過來也會擾亂你的心神。如果你吃得太少，饑餓感也會佔據你的大腦。你的身體應該處於一種完美的正常狀態，在沒有任何擾亂的情況下，你身體的自然狀態才能順利地工作。聲音應該盡可能地避免，因為它們會分散你的注意力。你現在已經把你大腦的指揮權交給了你的精神方面，而物質方面則處於服從狀態。開始時注意力很難集中，但隨著你的繼續，會變得越來越容易"。此段文字出自《The Children of Mu》最後一章。

Here is another way to practice concentration: "Relieve your brain of all material work. To do this a reclining or lying position is best. A position where every muscle in your body relaxes. This relieves the brain of looking after these parts of your anatomy. Cover your eyes, or close them so that no object strikes your attention; this is another relief to the brain. Do not eat too much or too little—both are bad. If you eat too much your stomach is overloaded and calls for brain work. If you have too little in your stomach hunger is occupying the brain. Your material body should be perfectly normal; nature should be working smoothly without a jar. Sounds must be avoided as much as possible as they divert the brain. You have now given over the command of your brain to the spiritual; the material is in subjection. Concentration is hard at first but becomes easier and easier as you continue." This passage is from the last chapter of "The Children of Mu".

[2] 憍陳如老師曾說過一段話，大致是：你需要擺脫憤怒、妒忌、誘惑，讓自己的內心平靜下來，智慧才能夠浮出水面。

Teacher Kaundinya once said something like this: You need to get rid of anger, jealousy, and temptation, and calm your heart, so that wisdom can surface.

7

不要讓"賺錢"佔據了你太多的生命
Don't let "making money" take up too much of your life

一個人如果以金錢為信仰，那麼他將永遠無法獲得真正的快樂。現代很多人都以金錢為信仰，而這是一個非常嚴重的錯誤。

If a person takes money as his "belief", he will never be able to obtain true happiness. Many people in modern times take money as their "belief", and this is a very serious mistake.

有的人會想我有了我想要的"豪車"我就會快樂，我有了我想要的"大房子"我就會快樂。

Some people think that if I have the "luxury car" I want, I will be happy; if I have the "big house" I want, I will be happy.

但事實並非如此，據調查發現，這些東西都有了的人們，好像也沒有真正獲得快樂。獲得這些物質，對他們來說，只不過是在朋友面前多了些談資而已，他們並沒有感覺自己有多快樂[1]。

But this is not the case. According to the survey, it seems that people who have all these things are not really happy. For them, acquiring these materials is just more topics to talk about in front of their friends, and they don't feel happy [1].

真正能讓人快樂的，只有內心在精神上得到充實，多做些有意義的事情才可以，比如：多感恩和幫助別人，多接觸和愛護自然，多聽些好的音樂，多給愛人些浪漫，多陪伴家人，等等。這樣你的靈魂才會感到滿足，精神層面也會得到提升，靈魂從此就不會再感覺空虛和寂寞。

What can truly make people happy is to be spiritually enriched and do more meaningful things, such as: being more grateful and helping others, getting in touch with and caring for nature more, listening to more good music, giving your lover more romance, spending more time with family, etc. In this way, your soul will feel satisfied, your spiritual level will be elevated, and your soul will no longer feel empty and lonely.

記住，生命中有很多重要的事情值得去做，而不能讓"賺錢"[2] 佔據了你太多的生命。

Remember, there are many important things worth doing in life, and you cannot let "making money" take up too much of your life.

注 Note

[1] 從物質上獲取的快樂，只會讓你快樂一時。而通過精神進步帶來的快樂，將會陪伴著你的一生。

The happiness obtained from material things will only make you happy for a while. And the happiness obtained from spiritual progress will accompany you throughout your life.

[2] 當你盡可能不再用金錢去衡量事物 "價值" 的時候，你的精神層面將會獲得很高的提升。

When you stop using "money" to measure the value of things as much as possible, your spiritual level will be greatly improved.

8

不要學別人的"錯誤"，而"污染"了自己的靈魂
Don't follow others' mistakes and end up polluting your own soul

當前的時代，隨著人們對金錢物質的欲望不斷變大，再加上各種負面信息的不斷影響，很多人都出現了性格浮躁，互相排斥，容易爭執的現象。

In today's world, as people's desire for money and material things keeps growing, and negative information keeps spreading, many people have become impatient, push others away, and often get into arguments

而在現實生活中很多人會想："他怎麼用惡語懟我，我就怎麼用惡語懟他。他如果對我使詐，我也會對他使詐。"其實，這是非常錯誤的做法。

In real life, many people think, "If he speaks harshly to me, I'll speak harshly to him. If he cheats me, I'll cheat him back." But this is a very wrong way to act.

別人怎麼對你是他的事，你怎麼對別人是你的事。

How others treat you is his business, and how you treat others is your business.

要記住：你可以用更合理的方式去對待事情，而不能學別人的錯誤做法，"污染"了自己的靈魂。

Remember: you can handle things in a more reasonable way, but you shouldn't follow others' wrong actions and pollute your own soul.

其實每個人都有自己的優點和缺點，需要互相包容，不能互相傷害。比如：別人有 100 個優點，但如果他存在一個缺點或因為某個話題跟你衝突過，你就要否定別人原來的那 100 個優點，進行無差別仇恨，這是不對的。

"In fact, everyone has their own strengths and weaknesses. We need to be understanding, not hurt each other. For example, if someone has 100 good qualities, but has one flaw or once disagreed with you on a topic, and you then deny all their good qualities and hate them completely — that is wrong."

你怎麼能保證自己做的也全是對的呢？所以我們要取長補短，多記別人的好處，多學別人的優點，找到自己的缺點，這樣才能在修行中得到進步。

How can you be sure that everything you do is always right? That's why we should learn from others' strengths, remember their good points, and find our own weaknesses. Only then can we truly progress in our personal journey.

"那別人總用惡語懟我，我氣不過就想把他懟回去怎麼辦？"

"What if someone keeps speaking harshly to me, and I feel so angry that I just want to talk back the same way?"

記得佛陀曾說過這樣一段話，大致是：「你送給別人禮物，如果這個人不接受，那這個禮物還是會回歸你自己。」同樣，別人對你的惡言惡語也是如此，如果有人懟你，你沒有接受，那麼這些惡言惡語還是會返給他自己。

I remember that Buddha once said something like this: "If you give a gift to someone and that person does not accept it, then the gift will still return to you." In the same way, if someone speaks harshly to you and you don't accept their words, those harsh words will return to them."

再加上因果法則是真實存在的，他傷害了你，給了你不好的感覺，那麼這個業力就會記到他身上，他也一定會受到處罰。可如果你以相同的方式去傷害了他，那麼你也就增加了這一個業力，所以不值得不是嗎？

Also, because the law of cause and effect is real, if he hurts you and causes you pain, that karma stays with him and he will face consequences. But if you hurt him in the same way, you only add to your own karma. So it's not worth it, right?

把內在的平靜交給自己吧，如果外界的"因素"能夠影響到你內在的平靜，那我們等於把平靜交給了別人，而不是自己。請記住，只要內心平靜下來，你就可以找到更合理的方式去對待當前這件事情。

Give your inner peace to yourself. If outside 'factors' can affect your inner peace, then you are giving your peace to others, not keeping it for yourself. Remember, once your mind is calm, you can find a better way to handle the situation.

9

只有學會調整欲望，才能獲得更多"幸福"
Only by learning to adjust your desires can you get more "happiness"

人只有學會調整欲望，才能在精神層面上得到提升。如果一個人的欲望過大，那麼這個人在生活中的"幸福感"就會被欲望減弱。

Only when people learn to adjust their desires can they be elevated spiritually. If a person's desire is too strong, then his "happiness" in life will be weakened by desire.

舉個例子：某人接到了一個任務，要求他每天用一個 500ml 容量的水杯去裝水，只要裝滿一杯水，他就能獲得"幸福值 +1"。但"欲望"到來之後，立刻給他增加了難度，水杯的容量被"欲望"擴大，這時他發現只有用 5000ml 容量的水杯裝滿一次，才能獲得幸福值 +1。隨著"欲望"不斷地要求變大，他不得不用 50000ml 容量的水杯，裝滿一次，才能艱難地獲得幸福值＋1。最後"欲望"把水杯的容量直接擴大到了 100000ml。這時他發現，不管他怎麼努力，都很難再去裝滿水杯裡的水。從此，這個人每次"裝水"都只感覺到了辛苦，也再沒有獲得原來的那些幸福值。

Here's an example: someone receives a task that requires him to fill a 500ml cup with water every day. Each time he fills it, he earns +1 happiness point. But then 'desire' shows up and increases the difficulty—the cup's size is expanded to 5000ml. Now, he has to fill a 5000ml cup just to earn the same +1 happiness point. As desire keeps growing, the cup becomes 50,000ml, and he struggles more just to fill it once. Eventually, desire enlarges the cup to 100,000ml. At that point, no matter how hard he tries, he can hardly fill the cup at all. From then on, each time he 'fills water,' he only feels exhausted and never gains the happiness he once did.

這就是為什麼現代很多人就算賺到了錢，也感覺不到快樂的原因。

This is the reason why many people nowadays do not feel happy even if they earn money.

舉的這個例子是為了讓大家明白，一味地擴大"金錢物質"的欲望[1]，將很難在精神層面上獲得提升。

This example is given to make everyone understand that if you blindly expand your desire [1] for "money and material things", it will be difficult for you to improve spiritually.

欲望的變大，反而影響了一個人正常幸福的獲取。

The increase of desire actually affects a person's obtainment of normal happiness.

所以人們應該適當地調整欲望，多做些有意義的事情，多認可自己，多分享和幫助他人，這樣你才能獲得真正的快樂，精神層面上才會得到相應的提升。

Therefore, people should appropriately adjust their desires, do more meaningful things, recognize themselves more, share and help others more. Only in this way can you obtain true happiness and achieve improvement on the spiritual level.

注 Note

[1] 貪欲過重的人，就像一個口渴的人在喝海水，結果喝下去的越多，越會讓自己感覺到口渴。

A person with excessive greed is like a thirsty person drinking seawater. As a result, the more he drinks, the more he will feel thirsty.

10

為什麼現在的生活物質豐富了，
你卻感覺不如"原來"的時候快樂？
Why do you feel less happy than before even though life
is materially rich now?

"人以肉體存在的唯一目的是發展靈性 [1] 。"

"Man exists physically for the sole purpose of developing spiritually." [1]

為什麼現在的很多電影融資高，特效多，明星雲集，可你還是會感覺不如原來的那些耐看？這是因為現在的很多導演、編劇，一切物質條件都很充足了，唯獨缺的是"拍出好故事的靈魂"。

Why is it that many movies nowadays have high financing, lots of special effects, and lots of stars, but you still feel that they are not as good as the original ones? This is because many directors and screenwriters today have sufficient material conditions, but lack the "soul to tell a good story."

同樣現代很多人都擁有了汽車，手機，房產等物質，卻還是感覺不到原來的那些快樂 [2] 。這也是因為多數的人"只顧著在物質上豐富自己，卻忽視了自己在精神方面的正確培養"。

Similarly, many people today own cars, mobile phones, real estate and other material things, but they still cannot feel the same happiness as before [2].This is also because most people "only care about enriching themselves materially, but ignore their correct spiritual cultivation."

"科技應當協助和支持心靈上的發展，而不該把自己禁錮在一個物質主義的世界裡 [3]。" 因為你最終會明白，只有你的 "精神內在" 獲得了提升，才是真正做到了提升 "自己"，只有這樣，你才能獲得真正的快樂和幸福。

"Technology should assist spiritual development, not confine people, more and more, within a materialistic world [3]." Because you will eventually understand that only when your "inner spirit" is improved can you truly improve "yourself", and only in this way can you obtain true joy and happiness.

注 Note

[1] 此句出自《海奧華預言》第三章。

This sentence comes from the third chapter of "Thiaoouba Prophecy".

[2] 物質上獲取的快樂，只會讓你快樂一時。而通過精神進步帶來的快樂，將會陪伴著你的一生。

The happiness obtained from material things will only make you happy for a while. And the happiness obtained from spiritual progress will accompany you throughout your life.

[3] 此句出自《海奧華預言》第六章。

This sentence comes from the sixth chapter of "Thiaoouba Prophecy".

11

為什麼現在的很多歌曲也不如"原來"的耐聽了？
Why are many songs nowadays not as good as before?

　　大家是否發現還有一個奇怪的現象：原來的某些歌曲你聽了很多遍也不會煩，原來的某些影視你看過很多遍也不會膩。這是因為在過去的時候，作曲家和導演基本都是在為"精神靈感"去創作作品。

Have you noticed a strange phenomenon: you can listen to some of the old songs many times without getting bored, and you can watch some of the old movies and TV shows many times without getting tired of them. This is because in the past, composers and directors basically created works for "spiritual inspiration".

　　而現在的很多歌曲，你很難去喜歡一個月。現在的很多電影看過一遍，你很難再去看第二遍。這也是因為現在大多數作曲者和導演，更多是為了"爆紅賺錢和票房賺錢"去創作作品。

Many songs nowadays, you can hardly go like for a month. And you can hardly watch a movie for a second time after you've watched them once. This is also because most composers and directors now create works more for the purpose of making money.

你要明白一切事物只要是以 "金錢" 為中心所產生的，就一定不會長久。只有為精神層面創作的作品 [1]，才能經典永恆。

You should understand that anything that is created by "money" will definitely not last long. Only works created for the spiritual aspect [1] can be classic and eternal.

音樂如此，電影如此，愛情友情更是如此。

This is true for music, for movies, and even more so for love and friendship.

注 Note

[1] 當前還有很少一部分創作者是單純在為精神靈感去創作作品，而大部分的創作者受 "物質主義" 的影響，在自己的靈性方面已經普遍出現了不同程度的降低。如果 "物質主義" 在一個人的心中佔據了主導地位，那麼他的 "精神方面" 就無法運作。正如 《The children of Mu》 中所寫的那樣："物質主義控制著人去積累財富，在他得到之後，又不得不在物質主義的思想驅動下去小心翼翼地照看他的財富以防止失去，這樣他就沒有時間來使他的精神方面得到成長"。因為一個創作者只有在精神方面得到了提高，他才能創作出更多好的作品。未來的人們如果都能認識到這一點，那麼好的作品一定會越來越多。

Currently, there are still a small number of creators who create works purely for spiritual inspiration, while most creators are influenced by "materialism" and their spirituality has generally declined to varying degrees. If "materialism" takes the leading position in a person's mind, then his "spiritual aspect" cannot act. As written in 《The

Children of Mu》 : "Materialism controlled the man to accumulate the wealth. The care of it after he has got it necessitates materialism to prevent his losing it, so that he has no time to improve the spiritual ". Because only when a creator is improved spiritually can he create more good works. If people in the future can realize this, there will be more and more good works.

12

你感興趣的，"後臺"都會推送給你，生活中也類似
Anything you're interested in, the "backend" will push it to yo, which is similar to the situation in life.

刷短視頻時，感興趣的視頻你會點贊，相應地，後臺會給你推薦更多你感興趣的視頻，後臺不會分視頻的品質如何，都會推給你，因為你感興趣。

When browsing short videos, you will like the videos that interest you. Correspondingly, the backend will recommend you more videos that interest you. The backend will not distinguish the quality of the videos, but will push them to you because you are interested.

同樣，我們也可以把"宇宙"看作一個龐大的數據庫，在"宇宙"看，事情沒有"好壞"之分，如果你的思想總是陰暗的，消極的，那麼你日常遇到的事情，也多是陰暗的複雜的。

Similarly, we can also view the "universe" as a vast database. From the perspective of the "universe", things have no distinction of "good or bad". If your thoughts are always dark and negative, then the things you encounter in your daily life are mostly dark and complex.

相反，如果你的思想總是維持在正面的積極的，那麼你所遇到的事情也會更多是正面的順利的。一個人的日常生活，會被一個人長期的“精神思想映射”所影響。

On the contrary, if your thoughts are always positive, then the things you encounter will be more positive and smooth. A person's daily life will be affected by his long-term "spiritual projection".

所以你有必要時常檢驗自己的心態，及時更正自己的想法，因為這可以增加你日常生活的好運和順利。而且經常保持正向的思維，也可以提高自身的振動頻率，自身的振動頻率有時會吸引相應振動頻率的事物，出現在自己的世界裡。

Therefore, it is necessary for you to check your own mindset and correct your thoughts in time, because this can increase the good luck and smoothness of your daily life. Also, by keeping a positive mindset, you can increase your vibrational frequency, and your vibrational frequency will attract things with the corresponding vibrational frequency to appear in your world.

13

請時刻提醒自己，你要做的事情還有很多！
Please always remind yourself that there are still many things you need to do!

人以肉體存在的唯一目的是發展靈性。

Man exists physically for the sole purpose of developing spiritually.

而現代人過度依賴"手機，平板"等電子產品，是消耗個人精神力的做法。你是否發現昨天"刷到"的內容，今天基本全部忘記？

Modern people rely too much on electronic products such as "mobile phones and tablets", which will consumes their personal spiritual energy. Do you find that you have forgotten all the content that you have "browsed" yesterday?

這就是信息不斷覆蓋產生的結果，大腦也有"緩存"，你不斷地刷手機，玩平板，大腦就會積累過多的垃圾信息、凌亂信息，長期以來，大腦的閱讀力和想像力都會發生不同程度的退化。

This is the result of the continuous coverage of information. The brain also has a "cache". If you keep browsing your mobile phone and playing tablet, your brain will accumulate too much junk and messy information. For a long time, your brain's reading ability and imagination will be degraded to varying degrees.

現代很多人無法耐心看完一本書、一部電影，甚至幾行字都很難看下去，這都是某些軟件的"瞬時欲望滿足"所造成的不良影響。

Nowadays, many people cannot patiently finish reading a book or a movie, and even find it difficult to read a few lines of text. This is the adverse effect caused by the "instant desire satisfaction" of certain software.

舉個例子：一個賣毒品的商人，不會考慮一個吸毒的人會變成什麼樣，他考慮的是如何賣掉更多的毒品。同樣，一個讓你上癮的軟件開發商，它不會考慮你的大腦是否正在退化，它考慮的是如何增加流量賺取更多的錢。

For example, a drug dealer doesn't think about what a drug addict will become, he thinks about how to sell more drugs. Similarly, a software developer who makes you addicted will not consider whether your brain is deteriorating, but how to increase traffic and earn more money.

但你必須為自己負責！請時刻提醒自己：放下手中的電子產品，站起身來，你要做的事還有很多！

But you must be responsible for yourself! Please always remind yourself: Put down the electronic products in your hand and stand up. There are still many things you need to do!

14

請避免不良信息"寫入"你的大腦
Please avoid having bad information "written" into your brain

地球人類之所以變得浮躁，與當下科技的發展有一定的關係。

The reason why people on earth have become impetuous is partly related to the development of science and technology.

很多關於暴力、慘案、汙穢等的不良視頻，充斥著網絡，如果刷到，請一定要點"不感興趣"，或儘快劃走，更不能傳播這些內容[1]。

There are many videos about violence, tragedy, filth, etc. on the Internet. If you see them, please click "not interested" or swipe away as soon as possible, and do not spread them. [1]

雖然這些內容與你本人沒什麼關係，但視頻裡的圖像已經對你造成了影響，有時在數小時，或數天內，你腦海中都會浮現出這些畫面，而這些畫面顯然對你的"靈體"造成了污染。

Although these contents have nothing to do with you personally, the images in the video have already affected you. Sometimes these images will appear in your mind within hours or days, and these images obviously pollute your "soul".

長期以來會使你性格暴躁，辦事效率低，幸運值減少。

Over time, it will make you irritable, inefficient and reduce your luck.

例如：路邊有兩個陌生人正在發生爭吵，互相謾罵，雖然這個事情與你無關，但那些聲音已傳到了你的耳中，影響到了你。

For example, there are two strangers quarrelling by the roadside, abusing each other. Although this matter has nothing to do with you, those voices have already reached your ears and affected you.

所以一個人如果想獲得提升，那麼你就要避免更多的不良畫面和信息，雖然你有時會忍不住想看想聽，但還是要克制自己，因為它可能會污染你的靈體。

So if a person wants to be elevated, then you have to avoid more bad images and information. Although you sometimes can't help wanting to see and hear them, you still have to restrain yourself because it may pollute your Astral body.

注 Note

[1] "應該報導那些能提高人們心智的、有意義的事件，而不是用負面信息給他們洗腦。" 此句出自《海奧華預言》第九章。我們每個人都應該傳播積極的、正能量的事件，而不能傳播那些負面的信息，因為你的一個不經意的傳播很可能會讓另一個人對此事件進行模仿。

"There are so many worthwhile things to show - reports of worthwhile events which improve the psyche of Earth people rather than brainwashing them in a negative way." This sentence comes from the ninth chapter of "Thiaoouba Prophecy". Each of us should spread positive events instead of negative information, because one of your casual spreads is very likely to make another person imitate this event.

15

人的一生，就是為了體驗"生活中的過程"
life is about experiences

人的一生，其實就是為了要體驗所有事情的過程 [1]。

A person's life is actually about experiencing everything [1].

當下的時代，某些科技過度地簡化"過程感"，最直接的結果就是人類越來越懶惰，靈性越來越降低。

In today's era, certain technologies overly simplify the "sense of process", and the most direct result is that human beings are becoming more and more lazy and their spirituality is declining.

舉個例子，你需要買件衣服，如果你去逛街，一家一家去店鋪試穿，最後買到了自己喜歡的衣服。這種情況下，你會體驗"經歷過程"後的滿足感，這件衣服你也會穿很久。但如果你是躺在家裡，在手機上選了某件衣服，快遞到家後就算這件衣服是你喜歡的，但精神上的滿足也會大打折扣，衣服自然也不會跟你多久。原因是你省掉了很多的"過程感"。

For example, if you need to buy a piece of clothing, you go shopping, try on clothes in every store one by one, and finally buy the clothes you like. In this case, you will experience the satisfaction of "going through the process" and you will wear this piece of clothing for a long time. But if you are lying at home and choose a piece of clothing on your mobile phone, even if you like the clothes when they are delivered to your home, the spiritual satisfaction will be greatly reduced and you will naturally not keep the clothes for long. The reason is that you skipped a lot of "process sense"

再舉個例子，你買來了蔬菜肉類等食物，自己切菜自己配料，製作完成後，在食用時你的那種滿足感會非常強烈，而且你也會很開心。但如果同樣的一道菜，你選擇的是"外賣"送到家中，那麼你的滿足感就會大打折扣，這也是因為你省掉了太多的"過程感"。

To give another example, you buy vegetables, meat and other foods, cut them and prepare the ingredients yourself, and after you finish cooking them, you will feel a strong sense of satisfaction when you eat them, and you will also be very happy. But if you choose to have the same dish delivered to your home, your sense of satisfaction will be greatly reduced, and this is because you have skipped too much of the "sense of process".

舉這兩個簡單的例子是為了提醒大家，不要被某些太便捷的科技"綁架"。不然時間久了，個人的靈性將會出現退化，大腦的思考能力也會減弱，工作效率也會變低。

I give these two simple examples to remind everyone not to be "kidnapped" by certain technologies that are too convenient. Otherwise, over time, the individual's spirituality will degenerate, the brain's thinking ability will weaken, and work efficiency will decrease.

所以請儘量避免或減少使用"太便捷的科技"，因為你需要為自己的未來負責。

So please try to avoid or reduce the use of "too convenient technology", because you need to be responsible for your future.

注 Note

[1] 人的一生就是來獲得體驗的，如以上兩個小例子還沒法讓你理解其中的意義，那請再看一下這兩段文字：

The purpose of life is to gain experience. If the above two examples still cannot help you understand the meaning, then please take another look at these two paragraphs:

比如你需要創作一件玉器，第一種情況是別人製作好了直接給你，第二種情況是給你一塊"原石"和"工具"，讓你自己雕刻出來。你感覺哪種情況會讓你獲得成就感？答案肯定是後者，因為你經歷了過程和體驗，所以你親手製作的這件"玉器"會更加富有意義，你會更加珍惜。

For example, if you need to create a piece of jade, the first situation is that someone else makes it and gives it to you directly, and the second situation is that you are given a piece of "raw stone" and "tools" and asked to carve it yourself. What kind of situations make you feel fulfilled? The answer is definitely the latter. Because you have gone through the process and experience, the "jade" you made by yourself will be more meaningful and you will cherish it more.

還有一個身邊的例子，你和朋友們一起去吃龍蝦，第一種方式是別人給你剝好了放盤子裡讓你食用，第二種方式是你自己動手去剝殼之後再食用，你感覺哪種食用方式的幸福感會更加強烈？答案肯定也是後者。因為你經歷了過程和體驗，所以你會獲得更多的幸福感。

Here is another example from our daily life. You go to eat lobster with your friends. The first way is that someone peels the lobster for you and puts it on a plate for you to eat. The second way is that you peel the shell yourself and then eat it. Which way of eating do you think brings a stronger sense of happiness? The answer is definitely the latter. Because you have gone through the process and experience, you will gain more happiness.

16

你能遇見的人，一般都有“原因”
There is usually a “reason” for the people you meet.

人的一生中會遇到各種各樣不同的人，然而多數的“遇見”都不是偶然。每個人的出現，或許早已為你存在了某些原因。

People will meet all kinds of different people in their lives, but most of the “encounters” are not accidental. Perhaps there have already been certain reasons for everyone's appearance.

很多人會把遇見的人大致分成兩類，一類是好人，另一類是壞人。

Many people roughly divide the people they meet into two groups: good people and bad people.

其實你應該換一種思維去理解：好人就是給你指導給你幫助的人，壞人就是給你磨煉給你考驗的人。

In fact, you should understand it in a different way: Good people are those who guide and help you, while bad people are those who train and test you.

當你的思想維度慢慢提高時，你將不會再用"好壞"區分遇到的人，去掉"好壞"以後，就只剩下了另外兩類人：一是給你指導的人，二是給你考驗的人。

As your thinking level gradually improves, you will no longer use "good" or "bad" to distinguish the people you meet. After removing "good" or "bad", only two other types of people will remain: one is the person who guides you, and the other is the person who tests you.

在你的靈魂逐漸被淨化之後，你又會發現，這一生中，只有這兩類人都出現，你才能取得更大的進步、成就和非凡。

After your soul is gradually purified, you will find that only when these two types of people appear in your life can you make greater progress, achievements and extraordinary accomplishments.

所以請感謝"高級自我"為你安排遇見的每一個人。

So please thank your Higher Self for everyone you meet.

精神層面提升進化 中級

Spiritual Level Ascension Evolution (Intermediate)

17

困難和誘惑同樣都是人生中的考驗
Difficulties and temptations are both tests in life

人的生活中，不止"困難"是一種考驗，而"誘惑"也是一種考驗。解決困難可以提升自己，抗拒誘惑也同樣可以獲得提升。

In our lives, not only "difficulty" is a test, "temptation" is also a test. Solving problems can improve yourself, and resisting temptation can also improve yourself.

比如有些成功人士或名人，在解決了多年的困難之後，變得有所成就。這時他的生活中，就會出現各種各樣的不良誘惑。

For example, some successful people or celebrities become successful after overcoming difficulties over many years. At this time, all kinds of bad temptations will appear in his life.

如果這個人沒有抗拒第一個誘惑，那麼就會有第二個，接著是第三個，等等。但時間久了他才會發現，接受這些誘惑正是他走向失敗的導火索。

If the person does not resist the first temptation, then there will be a second, then a third, and so on. But as time went on he discovered that accepting these temptations was precisely the cause of his failure.

人的一生就像在做答卷（試卷的題目其實是自己選的），如果有一道"題"你沒有做對，那麼過不了多久你就會碰到相似的題目，再讓你做一遍，如果多次這種題目你都沒有做對，接下來可能就要面對相應的懲罰。

A person's life is like answering a test paper (the questions on the test paper are actually chosen by yourself). If you don't get one "question" right, it won't be long before you encounter a similar one and have to do it again. If you don't get this kind of question right many times, you may have to face the corresponding punishment.

因為你的"高級自我"始終想讓你得到進步，想讓你在這一世中，修掉你該要修掉的內容。

Because your "higher self" always wants you to make progress, and want you to overcome what you should overcome in this life.

18

永遠不要"羨慕"或"鄙視"別人的生活
Never "envy" or "despise" other people's lives.

每個人需要學習的知識不同，所以不要羨慕或鄙視任何"他人的生活"。

Everyone needs to learn different knowledge, so don't envy or despise any "other people's lives".

很多人羨慕富有的人，而抱怨自己不富裕，或鄙視不富裕的人，這都是錯誤的。

Many people envy the rich and complain that they are not rich, or despise the poor. This is all wrong.

例如，有些人會抱怨[1]，我怎麼會出生在這樣的家庭？我家裡為什麼沒有別人家有錢？我的生活為什麼不如別人的好？等等。其實他們沒有明白，人的一生其實早已是"自己選擇"好的，命運（定數）安排的一切，都是為了讓自己能學到更多，每個人從"出生"起，就已定下了不同的使命。

For example, some people will complain[1], why was I born in such a family? Why is my family not as rich as other families? Why is my life not as good as others? etc. In fact, they don't understand that a person's life has already been "chosen" by themselves. Everything arranged by fate (predestined) is to enable you to learn more. Everyone has a different mission since birth.

所以，無論"高級自我"把你安排在什麼樣的家庭，都不要抱怨，你只要記住"不斷進步自己和修掉自己的缺點"就可以。

Therefore, no matter what kind of family your "higher self" arranges you in, don't complain. Just remember to "constantly improve yourself and overcome your shortcomings."

未來你會明白，往往"先抑後揚"的人生才是最有趣的人生[2]，才能讓你在本世學到更多的內容。

In the future, you will understand that a life that is "no sweet without sweat" is often the most interesting one [2], and it enables you to learn more in this life.

注 Note

[1] 人的內心之所以會感覺到生活中有痛苦，主要原因是存在這三點：第一，追求了錯誤的東西；第二，見不得別人比自己好；第三，過分追求他人對自己的認可。這也是因為大多數的人受物質主義的影響，只顧著向外看，而沒有向內尋。正所謂"不輕易評價別人是一種修養，不活在別人的評價中是一種修行"，而修行其實就是修自己的內心，與他人沒有太大的關係。如果一個人能夠試著向內看，找到自己的這三大根源，擺脫貪婪、妒忌和傲慢，那麼你的心靈將會從牢籠中得到解脫，幸福和喜悅會重新回

到你的內心。

The main reasons why people feel pain in life are: first, they pursue the wrong things; second, they cannot stand others being better than themselves; third, they excessively pursue recognition from others. This is also because most people are influenced by materialism and only look outward instead of inward. As the saying goes, "Not judging others easily is a kind of self-cultivation, and not living in the evaluation of others is a kind of spiritual practice." And spiritual practice is actually about cultivating one's own inner self, which has little to do with others. If a person can try to look inward, find these three roots of himself, and get rid of greed, jealousy and arrogance, then your soul will be liberated from the cage, and happiness and joy will return to your heart again.

[2] 人的一生就是來獲得精神體驗的，而更多的情況下你需要把"不和諧的"事物改變成"和諧的"，把"落後的"改變成"進步的"，等等，這樣才能在生活的過程中獲得更好的精神體驗。但記住一定不要跟別人比，因為你要對比的是昨天的"自己"。

A person's life is to gain spiritual experience. And more often than not, you need to transform the "disharmonious" into the "harmonious", the "backward" into the "progressive", and so on. Only in this way can you obtain a better spiritual experience in life. But remember never to compare yourself with others, because what you are comparing with is the "self" of yesterday.

19

"內在精神"和"表面物質"哪個更重要？
Which is more important, "inner spirit" or "external material"?

一個人如果只在"表面物質"上豐富自己，不在"內心精神"上得到進步，時間久了這個人將會迷失自我。

If a person only enriches himself in "external material" and does not make progress in "inner spirit", this person will lose himself over time.

比如：一個糕點師，越來越考慮如何豪華包裝產品，而不去提升"糕點"的內在品質，那麼他已經走錯了方向。

For example: If a pastry chef only considers how to package his products luxuriously but does not improve the quality of the "pastries" themselves, then he has gone in the wrong direction.

一部電影，導演越來越注重明星、特效，而不注重內在情節，那麼這部電影，到最後也很難變成經典。

If a director of a movie pays more and more attention to stars and special effects and less to the plot, then the movie is unlikely to become a classic in the end.

一支球隊，越來越注重外在補給，不去提升內在的素質，就算他們天天穿名牌，吃補品，那麼它也永遠不會是一支好球隊。

If a team pays more and more attention to external supplies and does not improve its internal qualities, it will never be a good team even if they wear famous brands and take supplements every day.

舉的這些例子是為了讓大家明白，一個人如果只在表面物質上豐富自己，而不去正確培養內在精神的話，那麼他就算獲取再多的物質，也不會得到真正的提升。只有提高了自己的"精神內在"，這個人才算是獲得了真正的提升。

These examples are given to make everyone understand that if a person only enriches himself in superficial material aspects, but does not properly cultivate his inner spirit, then no matter how much material he obtains, he will not be truly improved. Only when he improves his "spiritual inner self" can he be said to have achieved real improvement.

所以"人的一生不在於你能獲得多少金錢物質或地位，而在於你能獲得多少精神上的體驗和提升"。最終每個人都會明白：所有物質都只是暫時為你服務的"工具"，能獲得精神上的體驗才是"最終目的"。因為在輪回時，只有你的精神和靈魂會被帶走 [1]。

Therefore, "a person's life is not about how much money, material or status you can get, but how much spiritual experience and improvement you can get." In the end, everyone will understand that all material things are just "tools" that serve you temporarily, and gaining spiritual experience is the "ultimate goal." Because in reincarnation, only your spirit and soul will be taken away. [1]

注 Note

[1] 關於精神和靈魂的關係，在第 45 篇短文中，有詳細描寫。

The relationship between spirit and soul is described in detail in the 45th article.

20

你的健康程度與"精神層面"有關
Your health is related to the "spiritual level".

　　一個人在精神上獲得提升，能夠極大地影響這個人身體健康的程度。

A person's spiritual improvement can greatly affect his physical health.

　　現代人太注重身體的補給，不注重精神的培養，這也是錯誤的做法。

Modern people pay too much attention to physical nourishment and not spiritual cultivation, which is wrong.

　　例如，一個人天天吃補品，天天去醫療機構做保健，可他會發現身體並沒有得到本質的改善，反而會越來越依賴那些產品。這是因為此人只看到表面的身體出現了問題，卻沒有注意內在的精神也出現了問題。

For example, a person who takes supplements and goes to medical institutions for health care every day may find that his body has not been substantially improved, but will become more and more dependent on those products. This is because this person only saw that there was a problem with the body, but failed to notice that there was also a problem with the inner spirit.

相反你可以看那些，經常接觸自然，喜歡音樂，愛做公益的人們，他們並沒有吃太多的補品，也沒怎麼去醫療機構做保健，身體卻依然能保持著健康。

On the contrary, you can look at those people who often get in touch with nature, like music, and love to do public welfare. They don't take too many supplements, nor do they go to medical institutions for health care, but their bodies can still remain healthy.

這也是因為，這些人在精神上始終保持著補充，靈體就會充滿著能量，身體自然會保持健康。

This is also because these people are always replenished spiritually, and their spirits will be filled with energy, so their bodies will naturally remain healthy.

舉例是為了讓大家明白，我們都是有靈性的人類，關注表面的身體固然重要，但內在的精神則更加重要。

The purpose of giving examples is to make everyone understand that we are all spiritual human beings. While it is important to pay attention to the physical body, the inner spirit is more important.

21

色彩能夠影響一個人的"精神狀態"
Color can affect a person's "mental state".

大自然創造出豐富的色彩，這證明色彩一定有著特別的作用。

Nature creates rich colors, which proves that colors must have a special purpose.

實際上色彩能夠極大地影響一個人日常的精神狀態，不同的顏色能給人體帶來不同的"振動"。

In fact, color can greatly affect a person's daily mental state, and different colors can bring different "vibrations" to the human body.

那些總感覺自己沒精神，或身體不健康的人們，可以嘗試提升一下衣物的色彩，在家中和車內擺放一些帶有色彩的物品，這些色彩的振動會作用於你身體上的某些點，從而改善你的精神力。

Those who always feel listless or unhealthy can try to improve the color of their clothes and place some colorful objects at home and in their car. The vibrations of these colors will act on certain points on your body, thereby improving your spiritual energy.

例如，你屋裡的燈光如果是冷白色，那麼你就總會感到家裡冷清和沒有活力。但如果你換成了明亮的暖白色，那麼你就可以改善家裡的溫馨感和溫暖感，相應的心情也會轉好。

For example, if the light in your room is cold white, then you will always feel that your home is cold and lifeless. But if you switch to bright warm white, then you can improve the sense of warmth and coziness in your home, and your mood will also improve accordingly.

舉例是為了讓大家明白，你平常不在乎或沒注意的色彩，它正在或多或少地影響著你。

The purpose of giving examples is to make everyone understand that the colors that you usually don't care about or pay attention to are affecting you to a greater or lesser extent.

日光是由 7 種不同的色彩組成，它在不斷地給萬物補充著能量，這足以證明色彩的振動擁有著特殊能量 [1]。

Sunlight is composed of 7 different colors, which constantly replenishes energy for everything. This is enough to prove that the vibration of color has special energy.[1]

所以請適當利用色彩，改善和補充自己的精神力 [2]，這將是個有效的做法。

So please use colors appropriately to improve and replenish your spiritual energy [2], and it will be effective.

注 Note

[1] 比如科學界已經證實了藍光和黃光對人體具有某些治療的作用，

而其他顏色的振動也一定會有特別的作用。

For example, the scientific community has confirmed that blue and yellow light have certain therapeutic effects on the human body, and vibrations of other colors must also have special effects.

[2] "如果你牆壁的顏色和你的氣場相匹配，你就能改善你的健康，或者保持良好的健康狀態。而且，這些顏色發出的振動對良好的心態非常重要，即便在你睡眠時它們也會產生影響。"此知識點可查閱《海奧華預言》第六章，有更多內容。

"By matching the colours of your walls with those of your Aura, you can improve your health or maintain good health. Further, the vibrations emanating from these colours are essential for good mental balance, exerting their influence even while you sleep."This knowledge point can be found in the sixth chapter of "Thiaoouba Prophecy", which is described in detail.

22

請"順隨自然，借助自然"，因為你是大自然的一部分
Please "follow nature and make use of nature", because you are part of nature

大自然已經為人類創造出一切可治療疾病的植物，目的就是讓人類不斷探索自然的奧秘，以提升自己的靈性。

Nature has created all kinds of plants that can cure diseases for humans. The purpose is to allow humans to continue to explore the mysteries of nature and improve their spirituality.

大自然創造的一切，都是與自然界和諧存在的。

Everything created by nature is in harmony with nature.

黃種人在遠古時期就已掌握了醫學和病理學，利用大自然給予的植物治療疾病，來達到治癒的目的，這是借助自然、順隨自然的做法。

The yellow race has mastered medicine and pathology in ancient times, using plants given by nature to treat diseases and achieve the purpose of healing. This is an approach that relies on and follows nature.

而現代大多數人的做法顯然與"順隨自然"相反，他們多數採用的是"對抗"的方式來治療疾病。然而"暴力對抗"產生的一切結果，都會是短暫的。這就是為什麼某些抗生素、激素等人工合成的藥品，總是立竿見影，但過不了一段時間病情又會捲土重來的原因。

The practice of most people today is obviously the opposite of "following nature". Most of them use "confrontation" to treat diseases. However, all the results of "violent confrontation" will be short-lived. This is why some synthetic drugs such as antibiotics and hormones always have immediate effects, but the disease will come back after a while.

所以，未來我們一定要瞭解自然，順隨自然，借助自然的力量，來達到我們想要的目的 [1]，而不是總想著怎麼去對抗。

Therefore, in the future we must understand nature, follow nature, and use the power of nature to achieve our purposes [1], instead of always thinking about how to fight against it.

地球人類化學合成的補品藥品，表面看起來"成分參數"很高，但不一定就適合人體，只有大自然為人類創造的，才是最適合人類本身的。

The supplements and medicines chemically synthesized by humans on Earth seem to have very high "ingredient parameters", but they are not necessarily suitable for the human body. Only those created by nature for humans are the most suitable for humans themselves.

因為"你自己"就是大自然的一部分。

Because "yourself" is part of nature.

注 Note

[1] 這裏的 "目的" 是指我們身體恢復健康的目的，或是保持良好健康狀態的目的。當然想要達到這種目的，只是依賴藥物肯定是不夠的。

請記住："危險存在於一個人的生活方式中"。不良的生活方式會降低自身的振動頻率，而所有外來疾病的入侵，幾乎都與自身振動頻率的降低有關。

人體其實是被一個氣場和一個橢圓形的以太力（場）環繞着，後者是由一種被稱爲 Ariacostinaki 的振動組成（知識點可在海奧華預言第五章查到）。這些振動一直髮生着以保護你，保護你不被其他的 "中醫中所說的外邪" 入侵，你可以理解爲這種振動就像一個身體的 "防火牆"，它會主動防禦外來疾病的入侵。

然而想要提高這種振動的頻率，我們就要先提高自己的精神層面（見第 20 篇），保持良好的生活方式。只有這樣，我們才可以達到身體持續健康的目的。

The "purpose" here refers to the purpose of restoring our health or maintaining a good health. Of course, to achieve this purpose, just relying on drugs is definitely not enough.

Please remember: "the danger exists in the way in which one lives. ". An unhealthy lifestyle can reduce one's own vibration frequency, and the invasion of almost all external diseases is related to the reduction of one's own vibration frequency.

The human body is actually surrounded by an aura and an etheric etheric force (field) of oval shape, and the latter is composed of a vibration known as Ariacostinaki (the relevant knowledge can be found in Chapter 5 of "Thiaoouba Prophecy"). These vibrations are constantly protecting you from invasion by "exogenous evils" in traditional Chinese medicine. You can think of this vibration as a "firewall" for the body that actively defends against the invasion of disease.

However, if we want to increase the frequency of this vibration, we must first improve our spiritual level (see Chapter 20) and maintain a good lifestyle. Only in this way can we achieve the goal of sustained physical health.

$$23$$

"夜晚的睡眠"比你想像得更重要
"Sleep at night" is more important than you think.

"我們都有自由的意志，為了使靈性得到提升，我們應該自律[1]" 再次提醒了人們自律的重要性。

"We all have free will and it is up to us to discipline ourselves in order to improve spiritually. [1]" reminds people of the importance of self-discipline again.

現代大多數人總愛熬夜，第二天貪睡，無法自律地控制自己，這顯然也是違背自然規律的。

Most people nowadays always like to stay up late, oversleep in the next day, and cannot control themselves, which is obviously against the laws of nature.

夜晚的睡眠是件非常重要的事情。

Sleep at night is a very important thing.

首先，人體的各個器官在進行自己的"工作"時，時間是已經設定好的，你不能隨意打亂它們的工作安排。

First of all, when each organ in the human body is performing its own "work", the time is already set, and you cannot disrupt their working arrangements at will.

第二，睡眠其實就等於在給自己的身體"充電"，它會充分補充你白天所需要用到的精神力。

Second, sleep is actually equivalent to "recharging" your body. It will fully replenish the spiritual energy you need during the day.

第三，"高級自我"有時會在你高效睡眠的時候，給予你某些"指導和想法[2]幫助你解決日常遇到的問題。也就是說，你在高效睡眠時"接受的指導"，有可能會比你白天用大腦努力想到的辦法，還要有效。

Third, your "higher self" will sometimes give you some "guidance and ideas" [2] to help you solve daily problems when you are sleeping efficiently. In other words, the "guidance" you receive when you are sleeping efficiently may be more effective than the methods you think of with your brain during the day.

所以，在這個充滿"科技誘惑"的時代裡，人們應該更加自律，嚴格要求自己，克服自己的惰性，才能夠獲得提升。

Therefore, in this era full of "technological temptations", people should be more self-disciplined, strictly demand themselves, and overcome their laziness in order to achieve improvement.

正所謂"夜晚睡一覺，方法自然到"。從今天起，請規範作息時間，順隨自然，堅持下去，你會更加進步。

As the saying goes, "Night brings counsel." From today, please regulate your work and rest, following nature, stick to it, and you will make more progress.

注 Note

[1] 此句子引用出自《海奧華預言》第九章。

This sentence is quoted from the ninth chapter of "Thiaoouba Prophecy".

[2] "在睡眠的某些时候，你的高级自我可以召唤你的灵体去它那里：有时是给予指导或想法；有时则是用一些方法修复灵体，补充灵体的精神力量；或是在重大问题的解决办法上予以启发。为此，你有必要确保自己的睡眠不被扰人的噪音，或是日间不良印象导致的梦魇所干扰。"此知識點可查閱《海奧華預言》第六章，有詳細描述。

"At certain times during sleep, your Higher-self is able to call your Astral body to itself and, either communicate instructions or ideas, or to regenerate it in some way, replenishing its spiritual strength or enlightening it in regard to solutions to important problems. For this reason, it is essential your sleep is undisturbed by intrusive noise or by nightmares resulting from harmful impressions received during the day. "This knowledge point can be found in the sixth chapter of "Thiaoouba Prophecy", which is described in detail.

24

"精神"上的建立，決定"事業"上的成功
Spiritual strength determines success in one's career

一個人只有在"精神上正確建立"，才能有未來事業上的成功。

Only when a person builds true spiritual strength can they succeed in their future career.

無論是一個企業，還是個人，首先要考慮的是如何把事情做好，提升自己的品德[1]或企業的內在品質，而後才能考慮賺錢。

Whether it is a company or an individual, the first thing to consider is how to do things well, improve one's own moral character [1] or the intrinsic quality of the company, and then consider making money.

現在很多企業和個人都把"賺錢"放在了第一位，這也是錯誤的。你要明白，當一件事情用精神力做到極致的時候，賺錢只不過是你努力後應有的"附加值"。

Nowadays, many companies and individuals put "making money" first, which is also wrong. You have to understand that when you use your spiritual force to do something to the extreme, making money is just the "added value" you deserve after your hard work.

而任何事物如果是"以錢為中心"所產生的，它可能會短暫獲取收益，但未來一定不會長久。

And if anything is "money-centered", it may bring short-term profits, but it will not last long in the future.

你要明白，無論哪個家族或企業，能夠持續傳承下來的，一定不是"賺來的金錢"，而是那種"正確的精神"。

You have to understand that no matter which family or company, what can be passed down continuously is definitely not the "money earned" but the "right spirit".

而且不管你是在哪個行業或是在哪個職位，還請記住這三句話：不是能力越大，責任就越大，而是責任心越強，能力才會變得越強；如果你是一個有能量且有能力的人，那你就應該幫助和影響你周邊的人，沒有憑什麼；如果你想成功，你首先要學會平易近人；如果你已經成功，那你更要去學會平易近人。

And no matter what industry you are in or what position you are in, please remember these three sentences: It is not that the greater the ability, the greater the responsibility, but the stronger the sense of responsibility, the stronger the ability will become; if you are an energetic and capable person, then you should help and influence the people around you, for no reason; if you want to succeed, you must first learn to be approachable; if you have already succeeded, then you must learn to be approachable.

注 Note

[1] 這裡要引用《海奧華預言》第 9 章上面的一段話：“如果船長不僅知識淵博、經驗豐富、思維敏捷，而且還公正、誠實，那麼他的船員自覺盡力工作的可能性就會很大。歸根結底，是船長的內在品質，決定了他的指揮效率。”也就是說，如果你是一個企業領導或管理人員，你需要先提升自己的內在品質，才能獲得更高的指揮效率。

Here's a passage from Chapter 9 of "Thiaoouba Prophecy": "If, as well as being knowledgeable, experienced and quick thinking, the captain is also fair and honest, the chances are great that his crew will do its best by him. It is, ultimately, the intrinsic worth of the captain that will determine the effectiveness of his operation" That is to say, if you are a business leader or manager, you need to improve your inner qualities first before you can achieve higher command efficiency.

25

能获得别人尊敬的，永远是精神方面的
What can gain respect from others is always spiritual.

無論哪個國家或個人，能真正獲得尊敬的，永遠是精神方面的，而非物質方面的。

No matter which country or individual, what can truly gain respect is always the spiritual aspect, not the material aspect.

現代人太注重自己金錢、物質方面的追求，不注重精神層面的提升，這也是錯誤的。

It is also wrong for modern people to pay too much attention to their pursuit of money and material things and not to the improvement of spiritual level.

一個國家再富有，但"精神层面"如果不夠高，那麼周邊的國家就會對其產生更多的妒忌和憎恨，很少會得到鄰國的尊重和尊敬。

No matter how rich a country is, if its "spiritual level" is not high enough, the surrounding countries will have more jealousy and hatred towards it, and it will rarely be respected by its neighbors.

同樣一個人如果很有錢，但精神上卻很貧瘠。那這個人也只會引來別人的羨慕和妒忌，也很少會獲得別人的尊重和尊敬。就算有朋友的虛假恭維，那也只是看重了他的金錢，而金錢建立的所有關係，也往往都會是短暫的。

Similarly, if a person is very rich but spiritually poor, he will only attract the envy and jealousy of others, and will rarely be respected by others. Even if there are false compliments from friends, they only value his money, and all relationships established by money are often short-lived.

所以，無論哪一個國家或個人，在追求物質的同時，也一定要注重精神方面的培養，因為只有這樣，他才可以獲得真正的尊重和尊敬。

Therefore, no matter which country or individual, while pursuing material things, they must also focus on spiritual cultivation, because only in this way can they gain true respect.

同樣，一個人能被別人深刻記住的，也永遠只是"精神方面"的，而非"物質和金錢"方面的，你看那些被歷史記錄下來的"偉人"，就是一些很好的例子。

Similarly, what a person can be deeply remembered by others is always only the "spiritual aspect", rather than the "material and monetary" aspects. Just look at those "great men" recorded in history, they are some very good examples.

26

文明的世界就該用文明的方法去解決問題
A civilized world should solve problems in a civilized way.

因為每個國家的發展方向有所不同，所以每個國家都可以比作成 "公路上來回行駛的車輛"。

Because each country develops in a different direction, they can be compared to "vehicles traveling back and forth on a road."

當對面的車輛駛來時，如果你們選擇的是互相衝突，互相碰撞，那麼後果一定就是兩敗俱傷。

When oncoming vehicles approach, if you choose to conflict or collide with each other, the consequence will surely be mutual loss.

相反，如果你們選擇的是互相尊重，相互讓步，那麼你們就一定可以到達各自想去的地方。

On the contrary, if you choose to respect each other and make concessions to each other, then you will definitely be able to reach where you each want to go.

因為用暴力衝突解決的問題，永遠都不會有好的結果 [1]。唯有互相謙讓，互相合作才能真正做到和諧共存。

Because resolving problems through violent conflict will never have a good outcome[1]. Only through mutual humility and cooperation can we truly achieve harmonious coexistence.

比如某個國家總是想以武力施壓的方式去獲取利益，但這些利益到最後也會以不同的方式 "被全部收回"。雖然這個國家武器先進，很多的國家都怕它，可對它的恨意也會是一樣。因為一切用暴力解決的問題，都不會產生好的結果。"靠劍活著的人，終將被劍所殺。"

For example, a country always wants to gain benefits by using force, but these benefits will eventually be "taken back" in different ways. Although this country has advanced weapons and many countries are afraid of it, they will also hate it. Because all problems solved by violence will not produce good results. "He who lives by the sword will eventually be killed by the sword."

當下的地球人類，只有不斷提升自己的精神層面，才能真正到達屬於自己的 "文明"，而文明的世界就該用文明的方式，去解決各自目前遇到的問題。

Only by constantly improving their spiritual level can the current human beings on Earth truly reach their own "civilization", and the civilized world should use civilized ways to solve the problems they are currently facing.

注 Note

[1] "暴力不可能有好報，永遠也不會。相反，解決的辦法是愛和修養心靈。而且，當你排斥你身邊的人，如果你總不願意幫助那些你不喜歡的人，你就在促進你文明的瓦解。"這一段話出自《海奧華預言》第九章《我們所謂的文明》。

而這些道理也同樣適用於我們生活中的每一個人，其實每個人都有他"善"的一面，就算是所謂的惡人，也是因為經歷了不公或積攢了怨氣而形成的惡。而一個惡人如果面對的是一個真正善良的人，他是會被改變的。但這個惡人如果面對的是一個與他暴力對抗的人，他就會變得更惡。

這就是，暴力對抗不會有好報的原因。

用"一堆火"永遠無法滅掉另外"一堆火"，因為火只能用水才能澆滅。同樣，佛陀也曾說過："仇恨戰勝不了仇恨，仇恨只有愛才能化解，這也是自然法則。"

"Violence does not pay, and never will. The solution lies, rather, in love and the cultivation of minds. When you push away your neighbours, if you aren't always ready to help even those whom you don't like, you contribute to the disintegration of your civilisation. "This passage comes from the ninth chapter "Our so-called civilization" of "Thiaoouba Prophecy".

These principles also apply to everyone in our lives. In fact, everyone has his "good" side. Even the evil people are evil because of the injustice they have experienced or the resentment they have accumulated. If an evil person faces a truly kind person, he will be changed. But if this evil person faces someone who violently confronts him, he will become even more evil.

This is why violent confrontation will not be rewarded.

Fire can never put out another fire, because fire can only be put out with water. Similarly, Buddha once said: "Hatred cannot defeat hatred, and hatred can only be resolved by love. This is also the law of nature."

27

每一個靈性生命，都要常去"有靈性"的地方
Every spiritual being should often go to "spiritual" places

人類被創造出精緻的五官，目的就是為了感受這世界的美好，來滿足精神上的體驗。

Humans were created with delicate facial features for the purpose of feeling the beauty of the world and satisfying spiritual experiences.

而現代大部分人只忙於賺錢或躺在家刷手機，不經常接觸大自然，或許早已違背了作為"靈性生命"的使命。

However, most people today are busy making money or lying at home browsing their phones and do not often come into contact with nature. They may have already violated their mission as "spiritual beings."

試想一下，你到達了一個自己很喜歡的自然景區，用眼睛欣賞著周圍風景的美麗，耳機裡播放出一首優美的音樂，同時呼吸著自然界純淨的氣息，最後又品嘗了一下你很喜歡的食物……

Imagine that you have arrived at a natural scenic spot that you like very much, and you appreciate the beauty of the surrounding scenery with your eyes, play a beautiful piece of music in your headphones, breathe in the pure air of nature, and finally taste your favorite food...

在這種情況下，你的靈體會獲得很大的滿足感，靈體的電子[1]也會因"這些美好"而感到受益，從而會給物理身體進行優化，讓人體變得更健康。

In this case, your Astral body will gain a great sense of satisfaction, and the electrons in the Astral body[1] will also benefit from "these good things", thereby optimizing the physical body and making it healthier.

所以，適當地接觸大自然、感受美好[2]，會對身心帶來非常有益的改善。

Therefore, getting in touch with nature appropriately and experiencing its beauty [2] can bring about very beneficial improvements to both the body and mind.

生命中有很多有意義的事值得去做，而不能讓"賺錢"佔據了你太多的生命。

There are many meaningful things in life worth doing, and you can't let "making money" occupy too much of your life.

請記住，你是一個"有靈性的人"，就要經常去有"靈性的地方"[3]，而不能總待在辦公的區域，做一台只會工作的"機器"。

Please remember that if you are a "spiritual person", you should often go to "spiritual places" [3] instead of staying in the office all the time and being a "machine" that only knows how to work.

注 Note

[1] 靈體（靈魂、星光體）是由大約 40 萬億億個電子組成，它正好與你的物理外觀相匹配。知識點出自《海奧華預言》第十三章。

The human Astral body (soul) is composed of about 4 billion trillion electrons, which just matches your physical appearance. The knowledge point comes from chapter 13 of "Thiaoouba Prophecy".

[2] 很多人會想，我天天工作很忙，也沒有錢去旅遊那怎麼辦？其實你不必去一個很遠的地方，在你的身邊就有很多"免費的美好"，只是你需要用心發現它們。

Many people would think, "I am very busy at work every day and I don't have money to travel, so what should I do?" In fact, you don't have to go to a very far place, there are many "free beauties" around you, you just need to discover them with your heart.

[3] 比如：一顆種子，無論你把它尖端朝哪地埋在土中，它總能知道向上生長就可以獲得陽光和能量。一顆向日葵，雖然沒有眼睛，但它總能知道太陽的走向，向陽而生。還有很多例子不再一一列舉，每一種動植物都有自己的靈性表現。大自然中充滿了靈性生命，而我們也是大自然的一部分，應當經常回到自然的懷抱去感受美好。

For example: a seed, no matter where you bury it in the soil, it always knows to grow upward to get sunlight and energy. A sunflower, although it has no eyes, always knows where the sun is and grows towards it. There are many more examples, and I won't list them one by one. Every plant and animal has its own spiritual expression. Nature is full of spiritual life, and we are also part of nature. We should often return to the embrace of nature to feel its beauty.

28

音樂可以反映出一個人的精神內在
Music can reflect a person's inner spirit

音樂可以反映出一個人的精神內在，這是因為聲音的振動會通過雙耳直達人們的靈體，而在"精神進化"層面，不同的音樂 [1]，會對不同"精神進化程度"的人，產生不同情況的共振影響。

Music can reflect a person's inner spirit, because the vibrations of sound can reach people's Astral bodies directly through their ears. At the level of "spiritual evolution", different music [1] will produce different resonance effects on people with different "levels of spiritual evolution".

這也是為什麼有些音樂你聽了會很舒服，而有些人聽了會感到反感的原因。其實這種舒服，是音樂與此人當下的"精神進化程度"同頻共振的一種反饋。

This is also why you feel comfortable when listening to some music, while others feel disgusted. In fact, this kind of comfort is a kind of feedback that the music resonates with the person's current "level of spiritual evolution".

比如，一個愛聽"某些種類音樂"的人，如果遇到了一個和

他一樣 "喜歡同類音樂" 的人，那麼他們在其他興趣愛好或事物價值觀上也可以出現很多的相似。這種情況的根本在於，他們當下的精神進化程度較為接近，也可以說是他們的靈體 "振動頻率" 較為接近。

For example, if a person who likes to listen to "certain kinds of music" meets someone who likes the same kind of music, then they may have many similarities in other hobbies or values. The root of this situation is that their current spiritual evolution levels are relatively close, or in other words, their Astral bodies' "vibration frequencies" are relatively close.

所以，用音樂去檢測一個人和另一個人是否同頻，有時這也是一個簡單有效的方法。

Therefore, it is sometimes a simple and effective method to use music to detect whether one person and another person are on the same frequency.

注 Note

[1] 而且一個人說話的聲音和對音樂的欣賞水準程度，也幾乎可以反映出一個人的精神內在。關於聲音的重要性，在第 38 篇短文中，有詳細描寫。

Moreover, a person's voice and the level of their appreciation of music can almost reflect a person's inner spirit. The importance of sound is described in detail in the 38th article.

29

不要讓過多的金錢和物質，影響了你的下一代
Don't let too much money and material possessions affect your next generation.

金錢和物質的過多給予，會影響一個兒童正常靈性的發展；

Excessive giving of money and material possessions can affect a child's normal spiritual development;

現代很多人，不斷地在物質上滿足自己的孩子，只要是他想要的，什麼都願意給他買，總以為讓自己的孩子能比其他孩子物質上更充實，就是對自己孩子的"愛"。

Many people today constantly satisfy their children materially. They are willing to buy whatever they want, thinking that making their children more materially fulfilled than other children is their "love" for their children.

但更多的情況下，這種"愛"，反而會影響一個兒童或青少年正常靈性的發展。

But in more cases, this kind of "love" will affect the normal spiritual development of a child or teenager.

比如，一個孩子的玩具玩損壞了，如果家長協助孩子一起修理玩具，那麼"修好玩具"所經歷的過程，就會讓這個孩子在靈性上得到提升，他在以後遇到相似的問題時，就會主動想辦法，主動找方法。

For instance, if a child's toy gets damaged and the parents help the child fix it together, the process of "fixing the toy" will elevate the child's spirituality. When encountering similar problems in the future, the child will take the initiative to think of solutions.

但如果這個玩具玩壞後，家長每次都直接用錢給他買新的。那麼時間久了，這個孩子就會自然而然地以為"只要壞了，爸媽就能用錢買新的"，從而不願意去鍛煉自己動手動腦的能力，靈性上就不會得到鍛煉和提升。

But if the parents buy a new toy every time the toy breaks, then over time, the child will naturally think that "as long as it breaks, parents can buy a new one", and will be unwilling to exercise their hands-on and brain-power abilities, and will not be trained and improved spiritually.

舉的這個例子，是為了讓大家明白，如果你現在是一個相對"富裕"的家長，請儘量不要讓你的孩子知道你是"富裕"的。他如果在金錢和物質方面太容易得到滿足，他就不會在某些階段學到他應該學習的"知識"。

This example is to make everyone understand that if you are a relatively "affluent" parent, please try not to let your children know that you are "affluent". If he is too easily satisfied in terms of money and material things, he will not learn the "knowledge" he should learn at certain stages.

所以，在這個 "物質過剩，精神貧瘠" 的時代裡，我們要時刻提醒自己保持清醒的大腦，要正確地培養孩子的 "基礎能力"，不能因過多的金錢或物質，影響了他本該發展的 "優秀和靈性"。

Therefore, in this era of "material surplus and spiritual poverty", we must always remind ourselves to keep a clear mind and correctly cultivate our children's "basic abilities". We must not allow too much money or material to affect their "excellence and spirituality" that they should develop.

30

請愛護宇宙為我們精心設計的生態系統
Please protect the ecosystem that the universe has carefully designed for us.

一個人開始愛護自然環境時，他的精神境界即可以獲得很高的提升。

When a person begins to protect the natural environment, his spiritual level can be greatly improved.

人類生活在地球上，可以比作所有的人生活在一個舒適的帳篷裡，"帳篷"每天為人們抵禦著嚴寒和酷熱，裡面精密的調節系統，每天也在控制著溫度和濕度，補充著氧氣和人們所需的給養。

Human beings living on the earth can be compared to all people living in a comfortable tent. The "tent" protects people from the cold and heat every day. The precise regulation system inside also controls the temperature and humidity every day, replenishing oxygen and the supplies people need.

然而帳篷裡的人，總是在製造垃圾，製造有害氣體，那麼帳篷本身的"過濾系統"就會遇到巨大的麻煩，隨之出現的負荷情況，進而導致了調節系統的失衡。

However, the people inside the tent are always generating garbage and harmful gases. As a result, the "filtration system" of the tent itself will encounter huge problems. The subsequent load situation will further lead to the imbalance of the regulation system.

時間久了人們發現：帳篷裡的溫度開始出忽冷忽熱的現象，補水系統也開始出錯，不按常規的量進行補水，要麼極多要麼極少。由於系統長期負荷運行，"硬件"也開始出現過熱現象，某些線路甚至會冒出"超載的火焰"。

Over time, people found that the temperature inside the tent began to fluctuate, and the water replenishment system also started to malfunction, not replenishing water in the usual amount, either extremely much or very little. Due to the long-term operation of the system under load, the "hardware" has also begun to overheat, and some lines may even emit "overloaded flames".

人們最後才懂得，原來污染了帳篷裡的環境，其實就是污染了他們自己。

People finally realized that polluting the environment in the tent was actually polluting themselves.

舉的這個例子是讓大家明白，愛護環境不是為了別人，而是為了你自己。

This example is given to make everyone understand that protecting the environment is not for others, but for yourself.

　　所以，請愛護自己的星球，愛護宇宙為我們精心設計的生態系統。

　　So, please take care of your planet and the ecosystem that the universe has carefully designed for us.

31

作為一名人類，請明白"最基本的職責"
As a human being, please understand the
"most basic duty"

人類必須愛護自然，沒有願不願意，因為這是作為一名人類最"基本的職責"。很多人看到這裡會想，愛護環境跟我有什麼關係，那看完以下短文你可能會有所理解。

Human beings must care for nature, whether they are willing or not, because this is the most "basic duty" as a human being. Many people will think when they see this, what does protecting the environment have to do with me? Then you may understand after reading the following short article.

比如，一個小學生，吃的、住的和用的，總會有父母給他準備好，他當然不會考慮家裡的空調、暖氣、供電等基礎設施是怎麼來的，也從不會在意這些東西會是怎麼來的。

For example, a primary school student will always be provided with food, housing and necessities by his parents. Of course, he will not consider how the air conditioning, heating, power supply and other infrastructure at home come from, and he will never care how these things come from.

然而，地球上多數的成年人和這個"小學生"的想法差不多。

However, most adults on the earth think the same way as this "primary school student".

很多人從不考慮氧氣的補充、溫度的調節、生長食物的土地，是怎麼來的，他們總以為是"理所當然"，所以在做任何事情時，也從未考慮過自然的感受。

Many people never consider where things like "oxygen supply, temperature regulation, and land for growing food" come from. They always take them for granted, so when doing anything, they never consider the feelings of nature.

但人們卻犯了一個很大的錯誤，大自然為人類提供的一切，都是為了讓人類擁有更舒適、更美好的生活，而地球人卻很少懂得珍惜。

But people have made a big mistake. Everything that nature provides for human beings is to make them have a more comfortable and better life, but people on earth rarely know how to cherish it.

也就是說，大自然給予的一切，你都可以使用，可以體驗，可以享受。但你絕對不能去破壞、去浪費、去污染，否則你將違反"自然法則"[1]。

In other words, you can use, experience and enjoy everything that nature provides. But you must not destroy, waste or pollute, otherwise you will violate the "laws of nature" [1].

假如有一天，你手裡有一個塑膠垃圾正準備往自然界丟棄，請心裡一定要想起這個道理：大自然其實就是我們的另一組"父母"，如果父母每天都想著給你最好的食物、最好的環境，那麼你真的忍心給你的父母有毒的、不能降解"的東西，讓她去消化嗎？

If one day you have a piece of plastic waste in your hand and are about to discard it into nature, please remember this: nature is actually our other "parent". If your parents think about giving you the best food and the best environment every day, then do you really have the heart to give your parents toxic and non-degradable things for them to digest?

所以你要明白愛護自然，並不是為了別人，而是為了你自己。

So you have to understand that caring for nature is not for others, but for yourself.

注 Note

[1]這裡要引用《海奧華預言》書中的一句話："在情況變得不可救藥之前，你們只剩下不多的年頭去阻止污染了。"從目前地球人類近些年遭受的災難來看，大自然對人類的懲罰似乎已經慢慢開始，可人類還在那自私地追求著自己的利益，毫無察覺。當邪惡的事情被大多數人認可，而善良的人都被看作有罪的時候，懲罰將加速到來。如果地球人類再不覺醒，待大自然徹底憤怒的時候，那將會比任何人想像的都要可怕，這絕不是危言聳聽。為了我們共同的未來，為了我們自己的子孫後代，請加入愛護自然環境的行列吧。

Here is a quote from the book "Thiaoouba Prophecy": "You have but a few years left in which to arrest the pollution before the situation becomes irreversible." Judging from the disasters that humans have suffered in recent years, nature's punishment on humans seems to have slowly begun, but humans are still selfishly pursuing their own interests without noticing. When evil deeds are accepted by the majority of people, while the good ones are regarded as sinful, punishment will come sooner. If humans on earth don't wake up, when nature is completely angry, it will be more terrible than anyone can imagine, and this is by no means alarmist. For our common future, for our own descendants, please join the ranks of protecting the natural environment.

32

如何提升自己的"氣場"?
How to improve your "Aura"?

　　每個人其實都有自己的"氣場"，氣場雖然用我們的眼睛暫時無法看到，但"氣場"高的人靠近你時，你會從內心裡感覺到它的存在。

Everyone actually has his own "Aura". Although the Aura can't be seen with our eyes for the time being, when people with strong "Aura" approach you, you will feel its presence.

　　然而，一個人想要提升自己的氣場 [1]，首先要做的就是提升自己的人品。

However, if a person wants to improve his aura [1], the first thing to do is to improve his moral character.

　　漢字中人品的"品"字由3個"口"組成，而"口"的意思，代表著口口相傳。

The Chinese character for "人品 (moral character)" is composed of three "口" (mouth), and the meaning of "口" (mouth) represents word of mouth.

舉個例子，有 1 人說這個人 "怎麼樣"，無所謂。2 個人說這個人 "怎麼樣"，也無所謂。但如果有 3 個以上的人說這人 "怎麼樣"，那這個人的 "品" 就慢慢建立了起來。

For example, if one person says something about this person, it doesn't matter. If two people say something about this person, it doesn't matter either. But if three or more people say something about this person, then this person's "character(品)" will gradually be established.

由此可見，一個人在現實生活中的點點滴滴，都在悄然建立著自己的 "人品和氣場"。

From this, it can be seen that every little thing a person does in real life is quietly building up their "character and aura".

所以，在這個 "物質過剩，精神貧瘠" 的時代裡，不要隨波逐流，要時刻保持 "正氣、正念、正行" 才可以。要記住："不要去做，你不想讓別人對你做的事情。"

Therefore, in this era of "material excess and spiritual poverty", don't just follow the crowd, but always maintain "righteousness, mindfulness, and righteous actions". Remember: "Don't do what you don't want others to do to you."

堅持原則，人品自然會有所提高，"氣場" 也會因你的人品發生變化。

If you stick to your principles, your moral character will naturally improve, and your "aura" will also change because of your moral character.

注 Note

[1] 更多氣場 / 輝光的知識點可查閱《海奧華預言》第六章，有詳細說明。

For more knowledge points of aura, please refer to Chapter 6 of "Thiaoouba Prophecy", which is explained in detail.

　　如果你相信輪迴的存在、相信人類不是由猴子演變而來、相信
這世界萬物都是被精心設計過的，那麼請繼續向後閱讀，一些更深
奧的知識，正期待與你相遇

If you believe in reincarnation, that human beings didn't evolve from monkeys, and that everything in this world has been elaborately designed, please read on, and some more profound knowledge is waiting to meet you.

精神層面提升進化 高級

Spiritual Level Ascension Evolution (Advanced)

33

你的缺點，就是這輩子最該要修掉的"課題"
Your shortcomings are the most important "lessons" that you should correct in this life.

每個人不斷地"轉世輪回"，都是為了讓自己變得更加完美。

Everyone keeps "reincarnating" in order to make themselves more perfect.

然而每一世的課題，也都是"高級自我"和你一起精心選擇好的，為的就是讓你改掉缺點，更加進步。

However, the lessons for each life are carefully selected by your "higher self" and you, so that you can correct your shortcomings and make further progress.

如果這一世的"課題"中，你需要修掉的內容包含"妒忌"，那麼現實生活中，你就會經常遇到讓你妒忌的人。

If the "lessons" you need to overcome in this life include "jealousy", then in real life, you will often encounter people who make you jealous.

如果你的"課題"中，需要修掉的內容包含"脾氣"，那麼現實生活中，你就經常會遇到惹你生氣的人 [1]。

If the "lessons" you need to overcome in this life include your "temper," then in real life, you will often encounter people who make you angry [1].

再如果你的課題中需要修掉的是"貪心"，那麼現實生活中，你又能經常會遇到勾起你貪婪的事情 [2]，等等。

If the "lessons" you need to overcome is "greed", then in real life you will often encounter things that arouse your greed [2], and so on.

這些"課題"中的考驗，如果你真正地完成了其中一項，那麼下一世就不會再讓你遇到同樣的問題。

If you truly complete one of the tests in these "lessons", you will not encounter the same problem in your next life.

但如果你沒有較好地完成其中的一項，那麼下一世你可能還會遇到相似的問題。

But if you don't do one of them well, you may encounter similar problems in your next life.

你要明白，這一系列的課題，都是為了讓你在靈性上得到鍛煉，靈魂進化上更加完美。因為你的"高級自我" [3] 始終想讓你得到提升，更加進步。

You must understand that this series of lessons is all for the purpose of training you spiritually and improving your soul evolution, because your "higher self" [3] always wants you to improve and progress.

注 Note

[1] 生活中難免會出現爭執，而出現爭執的時候，一般雙方都會想著讓自己能 "贏"。而如果非要分出個勝負的話，那麼先原諒對方的那個人，反而可以看作是 "贏" 的人。因為你所經歷的每一件事都可以看作是本世生活中的考驗，如果主動選擇了原諒對方，能讓自己的內心平靜下來，這個課題在 "高級自我" 看來，你做的就會是很好，靈魂進化上也會獲得相應的提升。

Disputes are inevitable in life, and when they arise, both sides usually think about making themselves "win". If a winner must be determined, then the one who forgives the other first can be regarded as the "winner". Because every event you experience can be regarded as a test in this life. If you actively choose to forgive the other party, it can calm your inner self. From the perspective of the "higher self", what you have done will be very good, and your soul will also evolve accordingly.

而如果你採用的是比對方更暴力的回懟方式，去解決此類問題，那麼這次就算你表面上獲勝了，可過不了多久你會發現，這種相似的 "課題" 就還是會讓你遇到，再讓你做一遍。

However, if you use a more violent response than the other party to solve such problems, then even if you win on the surface this time, you will find that you will encounter a similar "lesson" again before long and will have to do it again.

[2] 佛學裡所講的 "貪、嗔、癡、慢、疑"，就是指人的貪婪、嗔怒、癡迷、傲慢、猜疑。如果一個人能試著找出自己的這些缺點並努力修掉它們，那麼他的靈魂進化程度也將會獲得很高的提升。

The " 貪、嗔、癡、慢、疑 " mentioned in Buddhism refer to human

greed, anger, obsession, arrogance, and suspicion. If a person can try to find these shortcomings in himself and work hard to eliminate them, then the degree of his soul evolution will be greatly improved.

[3] 更多關於"高級自我"的知識點，可查閱《海奧華預言》第六章，有詳細解答，非常推薦閱讀。一個"高我"管理著九個靈體（靈魂），就像一個"太陽"管理著九顆行星一樣地運行著。"高我"會記錄著你所有的一言一行，你體驗到的所有感覺也會通過大腦傳遞給你的"高我"。仔細想想我們的頭髮為什麼基本向上生長？而且頭頂的發旋和星系的模樣基本相似，這或許也有著一定的原因吧。

For more knowledge about the "higher self", please refer to the sixth chapter of "Thiaoouba Prophecy", which has detailed answers and reading is highly recommended. A "higher self" manages nine Astral bodies, just like a "sun" manages nine planets. The "higher self" will record all your words and deeds, and all the feelings you experience will be transmitted to your "higher self" through your brain. Think about it, why do our hairs basically grow upwards? And the spiral at the top of our head is basically similar to the shape of a galaxy. Maybe there is a certain reason for this as well.

34

如何獲得"更高級別"的指引?請看到最後與個人有關
How to get "higher level" guidance? Please read to the end. It is related to the individual

為什麼這麼多年來，地球人類的科技始終沒有質的進步，火箭還是靠燃料推進，重物還是靠車船運輸，這是因為就目前地球人類的靈魂進化程度而言，暫時還不適合擁有更高級的技術。

Why for so many years, there has been no qualitative progress in the science and technology of human beings on earth? Rockets are still propelled by fuel, and heavy objects are still transported by vehicles and ships. This is because, as far as the evolution degree of human souls on earth is concerned, it is not suitable to have more advanced technology for the time being.

現在的地球人類如果擁有了更高級的技術，很多人只會想著如何賺錢，如何控制民眾，如何掠奪其他星球的資源。

If humans on Earth today had more advanced technology, many people would only think about how to make money, how to control the people, and how to plunder the resources of other planets.

在這種情況下，高級靈體是無論如何也不願轉世到地球，給地球人更多高級技術的指導的。

Under such circumstances, high-level spirits would not be willing to reincarnate onto Earth and provide more advanced technological guidance to humans.

舉個例子，一個先進的科學家，會把"核能"獻給一個充滿狂熱分子的國家嗎？答案是肯定不會。

For instance, would an advanced scientist dedicate "nuclear energy" to a country full of fanatics? The answer is definitely no.

高級科技對靈魂進化程度高的人而言，這就是強大的能源，可以造福社會，造福人類的資源。

For people with highly evolved souls, advanced technology is a powerful energy source that can benefit society and humanity.

而對靈魂淨化程度低的人而言，就成了強大的武器，掠奪他國的手段，威脅更多人的方法。

But for people with low levels of soul purification, it becomes a powerful weapon, a means to plunder other countries and threaten more people.

由此可見，二者的精神內在是不一樣的，所以使用"同樣的技術"去創造的產物也是完全不一樣的。

From this we can see that the spiritual essence of the two is different, so the products created using the "same technology" are also completely different.

這個道理同樣適用於個人，如果你想獲得"高級自我"或他人更高級的指導（他人就是所謂的貴人），那麼請先修正自己的內心，應充滿正念，刪除所有的邪惡思想，這樣你才能獲得"更高級別的指引"[1]。

The same principle applies to individuals. If you want to get higher-level guidance from your "higher self" or others (who are called savior), then please correct your own heart first. You should be full of positive thoughts and delete all evil thoughts. Only in this way can you get "higher-level guidance" [1].

注 Note

[1] 古人所說的"傻人有傻福"這句諺語也是有道理的，比如你有三個孩子，老大非常精明心計很多，老二很會算計從不吃虧，老三誠實守信、內心善良。如果你作為孩子們的家長，你最願意多照顧的會是哪個孩子？答案肯定是：老三。

同樣一個"高我"管理著九個靈體（靈魂），就像祂的九個"孩子"一樣，"高我"也會多願意照顧那個誠實、勇敢、善良、單純的孩子。所以你要堅持走正道，不要被社會上的某些不良風氣所影響。你不需要有太多的心計，保持內心的善良，堅韌勇敢的走正道，時間久了，自然就會獲得更多的"指引"，也可以理解為更多的"神助"。

The old saying "fortune favours fools" is also true. For example, if you have three children, the eldest is very shrewd and scheming, the second is very calculating and never suffers any loss, and the third is honest and trustworthy and kind-hearted. If you are the parent of these children, which child would you be most willing to take care of? The answer is definitely: the third one.

Similarly, the "higher self" manages nine Astral bodies (souls). Just like his nine children, the "higher self" will be willing to take care of the honest, brave, kind and simple child. So you must stick to the right path and not be influenced by some bad trends in society. You don't need to be too calculating, just keep your heart kind and stick to the right path bravely. Over time, you will naturally get more "guidance", which can also be understood as more "divine help".

35

你"看不見的"，或許才是最重要的
What you "can't see" might be the most important

很多人只相信自己能看得見的、聽得見的，把一切看不見的、聽不見的、解釋不了的都當成迷信，這也是非常錯誤的。

Many people only believe what they can see and hear, and regard everything that they can't see, hear and explain as superstition, which is also very wrong.

前方遠處有一塊完全透明的玻璃，你看不見它，但你不能說它不存在。

There is a completely transparent glass in the distance ahead. You can't see it, but you can't say it doesn't exist.

Wi-fi 信號就在你四周遊蕩著，你也看不見它，但你不能說它不存在。

Wi-fi signal is wandering around you, and you can't see it, but you can't say it doesn't exist.

天上的衛星在天天注視著我們，你又看不見它，但你不能說它不存在。"

The satellite in the sky is watching us every day, and you can't see it, but you can't say it doesn't exist. "

然而一個人的"靈體"（也叫靈魂），是真實存在的，你看不見它，但它卻是人體中最重要的一部分。

However, a person's "Astral body "(soul) is real. You can't see it, but it is the most important part of the human body.

如果你相信靈魂的存在，那麼請先瞭解一下這個道理：人的一生，不在於能把自己的"外表"[1] 打造得多麼"光鮮亮麗"，而在於能往自己的靈魂裡"寫入"多少有意義的信息。

If you believe in the existence of the soul, please understand this truth first: A person's life is not about how "glamorous" their "appearance" [1] is, but about how much meaningful information they can "write" into their soul.

對一個人修行來說，"看得見摸得著的 [2]"並不是最重要的，而最重要的反而是那些你"看不見摸不著的"。舉個例子，你手裡有一塊電池，那這塊電池最重要的地方，一定不是你看到的這塊"電池本身"，而是這塊電池裡，儲存了多少你"看不見"的能量。

For a person's spiritual practice, "what you can see and touch [2]" is not the most important thing; rather, what matters most are those that you "cannot see or touch". For example, if you have a battery in your hand, the most important thing about this battery is definitely not the "battery itself" that you can see, but how much "invisible" energy is stored in this battery.

關於靈體（靈魂、星光體），之後的文章會有詳細描寫。

About the Astral body (soul), later articles will describe it in detail.

注 Note

[1] 這裡的"外表"是指追求表面的物質生活。

The "appearance" here refers to the pursuit of superficial material life.

[2] "看得見摸得著"是指能獲取的物質。不是最重要，並不是指不需要。這裡意思是表達：物質只是"工具"，能獲得精神體驗才是最終目的。

"what you can see and touch "refers to the material things that can be obtained. "Not the most important thing "does not mean that it is not necessary. The meaning here is to express that material things are just "tools" and the ultimate goal is to gain spiritual experience.

36

萬物皆有靈(1)——這個"靈"其實就是指的"靈體"
Everything has a spirit (1)-this "spirit" actually refers to the "Astral body"

　　萬物皆有靈，這個 "靈" 其實就是指的靈體。但靈體（靈魂）到底是什麼？讀完以下短文，可能你會有所理解。

Everything has a spirit, and this "spirit" actually refers to the Astral body. But what is a Astral body? After reading the following passage, you may understand.

　　例如，你在公路上開車，那個手握方向盤操控著車輛的人，就可以看作是這輛車目前的 "靈體"，當然你在公路上也可以看到其他正在行駛的車輛，卻很難看到裡面正在駕駛車輛的那個人。

For instance, when you are driving on the road, the person holding the steering wheel and controlling the vehicle can be regarded as the current "Astral body" of this car. Of course, you can also see other vehicles moving on the road, but it is very difficult to spot the person driving the vehicle inside.

　　再比如，你在玩一個網路遊戲，你在電腦前操控著遊戲裡的那個人物。這時電腦前的你，就可以看作是現在那個遊戲人物的“靈體”。當然其他的玩家也在這個網遊中，他們也都只是能看到對方遊戲裡的人物，而很難看到電腦前操控遊戲的那個人。

For another example, you are playing an online game and you are controlling that character in the game in front of the computer. At this moment, you in front of the computer can be regarded as the "Astral body "of the current game character. Of course, other players are also in this online game. They can only see the characters in each other's games, but it's very difficult for them to see the person in front of the computer controlling the game.

舉的這兩個小例子，只是想讓人們更簡單地理解“靈體”的作用性和重要性。

The two small examples I give are just to make it easier for people to understand the role and importance of "Astral body".

而在現實生活中，一個人最重要的地方，也是在於這個人體內的“靈體”，靈體是由數以億計的電子組成[1]，它擁有強大的記憶能力和物理身體分區的能力，等等。

In real life, the most important thing about a person is the "Astral body" within the body. The soul is composed of billions of electrons [1], which has powerful memory ability and physical compartment ability, and so on.

靈體雖然無法用肉眼看到，但這是百分百真實存在的一部分，而且是一個人體內最重要的一部分。

Although the Astral body can't be seen with the naked eye, it is a 100% real part and the most important part of a human body.

注 Note

[1] "一個正常人類的靈體是由大約四十萬億億個電子組成，這些電子中的每一個都有一個記憶體，並且每個電子的儲存能力，都堪比普通城市圖書館滿滿的書架上面所有書中包含的信息。"具體知識點請查閱《海奧華預言》第十三章。地球上某些物理學家也發現了人體內的電子，有強大的儲存能力。

（靈體＝靈魂＝星光體）

"A normal human Astral body contains approximately four billion, trillion electrons. Each of these electrons has a 'memory' and each is capable of retaining as much information as is contained in all the books that fill the shelves of an average town library." For specific knowledge points, please refer to Chapter 13 of "Thiaoouba Prophecy". Some physicists on the earth have also discovered the electrons in the human body, which have strong storage capacity.

37

萬物皆有靈(2)——"靈體"都有哪些重要的作用？
Everything has a spirit (2)-What are the important functions of "Astral body"?

靈體是由數以億計的電子組成[1]，它包含了強大的記憶能力和物理身体分區的能力，等等。

The Astral body is composed of billions of electrons[1], which contains powerful memory ability and physical compartment ability, and so on.

在一個人或動物的靈體內，已"編寫"好所有的物理分區指令，比如，哪裡應生長出四肢，哪裡應出現雙眼、雙耳、毛髮，等等，支配著任何物理結構，出現在身體該出現的位置。

Within the Astral body of a person or animal, all physical compartment instructions have been "written", for example, where the limbs should grow, where the eyes, ears, hair, and so on should appear, controlling any physical structure and making it appear where it should appear on the body.

"如果沒有靈體的控制，就沒有一個靈性生命的發展。"

"Without the control of the soul, there is no development of a spiritual life."

舉個例子，科學家可以製造出一個和"真正雞蛋"物理成分完全一致的"人造雞蛋"，但這個"人造雞蛋"永遠不會孵化出小雞。這是因為，地球人類目前無法植入那一點最重要的、能控制生命發展的"靈體電子"。

For example, scientists can create an "artificial egg" that is exactly the same physical composition as a "real egg", but this "artificial egg" will never hatch a chick. This is because humans on Earth are currently unable to implant the most important "spiritual electrons" that can control the development of life.

還有目前人類發現的 DNA 鏈，也只是一種信息編碼的物理載體（類似於儲存盤），而真正往 DNA 鏈中寫入信息的，其實就是那些電子，也就是靈體。

The DNA chain discovered by humans is just a physical carrier of information encoding (similar to a storage disk), and what actually writes information into the DNA chain are the electrons, that is, the soul.

"靈體只能在精神上得到充實，而非物質上。[2]" 也就是說，你越改善自己的心智，越提升自己的精神層面，身體在各個方面越可以得到有益的提升。

"The Astral body can only be enriched spiritually, not materially. [2] "In other words, the more you cultivate your mind, the more you upgrade your spiritual level, and the more beneficial your body can be in all aspects.

注 Note

[1] "靈體是由數以億計的電子組成，它正好與你的物理外形相匹配。一個正常人類的靈體是由大約四十萬億億個電子組成，這些電子中的每一個都有一個記憶體，並且每個電子的儲存能力，都堪比普通城市圖書館滿滿的書架上面所有書中包含的信息。"具體知識請查閱《海奧華預言》第十三章，有詳細描述。（靈體就是我們所說的靈魂，也稱為星光體）

The Astral body is composed of billions of electrons, exactly marrying your physical shape . A normal human Astral body contains approximately four billion, trillion electrons. Each of these electrons has a 'memory' and each is capable of retaining as much information as is contained in all the books that fill the shelves of an average town library. "For specific knowledge, please refer to Chapter 13 of "Thiaoouba Prophecy", which is described in detail.

[2] "靈體是住在你肉體中的一個身體，它回顧和記錄著你在各次生命歷程裡所獲得的全部知識。它只能在精神上得到充實，而非物質上"。詳細知識點可查閱《海奧華預言》第六章，有更多內容。

"You have understood that the Astral body is a body which inhabits your physical body recalling and noting all the understanding acquired during the course of its various lives.It can only be enriched spiritually - not materially. "Detailed knowledge points can be found in the sixth chapter of "Thiaoouba Prophecy", and there are more contents.

38

萬物皆有靈 (3) ——如何保護靈體?又如何滋養靈體?
Everything has a spirit (3)-how to protect the Astral body?
How to nourish the Astral body?

　　上篇短文提到過，靈體是由數以億計的電子組成，而這些 "電子" 又擁有著強大的記憶能力和身體物理分區的能力。"物理分區" 其實就是指一個人的體型塑造、面容優化、各器官的營養分配，等等，控制著物理身體所有的體徵發展。

As mentioned in the previous article, the Astral body is composed of billions of electrons, and these "electrons" have powerful memory and physical body compartment ability. "Physical compartment ability "actually refers to a person's body shaping, facial optimization, nutritional distribution of various organs, etc. The Astral body controls the development of all physical signs of the physical body.

　　然而 "靈體" 只會在兩種情況下受到損害: "吸食毒品" 和 "某些噪音引起的振動"。毒品想必大家都知道，對身體和靈體的危害是最大的 [1]。同時 "噪音" 的振動對靈體的危害也是不容小覷的。

The Astral body can only be harmed in two situations: "drug use" and "vibrations caused by certain noises". As we all know, drugs are the most harmful to the body and spirit [1]. At the same time, the harm caused by the vibrations of "noise" to the Astral body should not be underestimated.

靈體的電子會被噪音產生的振動所擾亂，從而使靈體的"物理分區"功能失衡 [2]；時間久了，物理身體的很多方面就會受到不好的影響。

The electrons of the Astral body will be disturbed by the vibrations generated by the noise, causing the Astral body's "physical compartment" function to become unbalanced [2]; over time, many aspects of the physical body will be adversely affected.

那麼，影響了靈體電子會使"物理分區"失衡，相應的"滋養了靈體電子"就會使"物理分區"更加完善。

Then, affecting the spiritual electrons will cause the "physical compartment" to become unbalanced, and correspondingly "nourishing the spiritual electrons" will make the "physical compartment" more perfect.

比如，你靜下心來經常聽一些愉悅的純音樂，自然界的流水聲，叢林中鳥叫的聲音，等等，這些聲音產生的有益振動，就會優化和梳理你靈體電子的排列 [3]，從而使"物理分區"的功能更加完善和均衡。

For example, if you calm down and often listen to some pleasant pure music, the sound of flowing water in nature, the sound of birds singing in the jungle, etc., the beneficial vibrations generated by these sounds will optimize and sort out the arrangement of your Astral body's electrons [3], thereby making the function of "physical compartment" more complete and balanced.

顯然，傳到我們耳朵裡的聲音非常重要，甚至會比用眼睛看到的圖像還要重要 [4]。

Obviously, the sound we hear is very important, even more important than the image we see with our eyes [4].

由此可見，"好的聲音"，能對身體帶來非常有益的改善 [5]，所以適當地運用"聲音"來優化自己，這將是一個有效的做法。

It can be seen that "good sounds" can bring very beneficial improvement to the body [5], so it will be an effective practice to use "sounds" appropriately to optimize yourself.

注 Note

[1] "毒品有一種完全違反自然的效果。吸毒後，一個人的靈體就像在'睡'著體驗虛幻的感受，而這將完全破壞他的判斷力，這和一具肉體在經歷一場重大的外科手術時的情況相同。換句話講，這就好比一個工具因使用不當，或被用錯了地方而導致變形或損壞一樣。根據一個人受毒品影響的時間長短，他的靈體將衰退，或者更準確講，是被虛假數據浸透。靈體的"恢復"需要好幾世，所以無論如何都要避免毒品。"此段文字出自《海奧華預言》第九章。

"Considering only drugs, it must be understood that they have an influence that is totally against Nature. When drugged, an individual's Astral body is as though 'asleep' experiencing artificial sensations that completely distort his or her judgement. It is in the same situation as a physical body is during an important surgical operation. If you like, it's like a tool that we bend or break by using it incorrectly or for a task for which it was not intended. 'According to the length of time that a person is under the influence of drugs, his or her Astral body is going to decline or, more exactly, it is going to become saturated with false data. 'Recovery' for the Astral body can take several lifetimes: for this reason, drugs should be avoided at all costs.'" This passage is from the ninth chapter of "Thiaoouba Prophecy".

[2] "噪音會直接侵襲你靈體的電子，製造寄生振盪，在此我用了一個廣播電視術語。如果你在看電視螢幕並注意到幾個白斑，這表明一個小'寄生振盪'在活動。同樣，如果有人在你家隔壁使用電動工具，那些產生在你螢幕上的大寄生振盪將導致圖像被徹底破壞。同樣的事情會發生在靈體身上。但遺憾的是，你不能像看電視螢幕時那樣看到它們。而且，這是更糟的，因為噪音損害了你的電子"。此段文字出自《海奧華預言》第十三章。

"Noise directly attacks the electrons of your Astral body creating parasites, to use a radio and television term. If you are watching a television screen and notice several white spots, this is an indication that a small 'parasite' is at work. Similarly, if someone is operating an electric tool next door to your house, such large parasites will be produced on your screen that the image will distort completely. 'The same thing occurs with the Astral body, but unfortunately you won't be aware of it in the same way that you are with a television screen; and, it's much worse, since noise damages your electrons" This passage is from chapter 13 of "Thiaoouba Prophecy".

[3] 人的靈體（靈魂、星光體）是由大約 40 萬億億個電子組成，它的排列形狀正好與你的物理外觀相匹配。

The human Astral body(soul) is composed of about 4 billion trillion electrons, and its arrangement shape just matches your physical appearance.

[4] 我們可以做一個實驗：現在調整好你的坐姿，先把眼睛閉上，用心感受你周圍的世界十秒鐘，記下這個感覺。

然後，睜開眼睛，將你的雙耳用手堵住，再感受一下周圍的世界十秒鐘，也記下這個感覺。

這時你會發現，在這兩種情況下，後者比前者會更讓你感覺不舒服，雖然你的眼睛可以看到周圍的一切，但那種與世界隔絕的感覺會更加明顯。這是因為當你的雙耳被堵住之後，你的靈體已無法充分感覺到外界的振動，靈體就像被包裹住了一樣，所以才會有那種 "窒息感"。

由此可見，聽到的聲音比看到的圖像更加重要。

[4] We can do an experiment: now adjust your sitting posture, first close your eyes, feel the world around you for ten seconds, and remember this feeling.

Then, open your eyes, cover your ears with your hands, feel the world around you for another ten seconds, and remember this feeling too.

At this time, you will find that in both cases, the latter will make you feel more uncomfortable than the former. Although your eyes can see everything around you, the feeling of being isolated from the world will be more pronounced. This is because when your ears are blocked, your Astral body can no longer fully feel the vibrations of the outside world. It is like being wrapped up, so you will have that "suffocating feeling".

Thus, the sound you hear is more important than the image you see.

[5] 古代人把五音角、徵、宮、商、羽與人的五臟肝、心、脾、肺、腎來對應，用音樂來治療疾病，就是利用了聲音的振動來優化自身。而且一個人說話的聲音和對音樂的欣賞水準程度，也幾乎可

以反映出一個人的精神內在。

The ancient Chinese people associated the five-tone " 角、徵、宮、商、羽 " with the five human organs - liver, heart, spleen, lung and kidney. Using music to treat diseases is to use the vibration of sound to optimize oneself. Moreover, the tone of a person's voice and the level of his appreciation of music can almost reflect his inner spirit.

39

為什麼古人會說"一切皆有定數"
Why did the ancients say that "Everything is predetermined"

行星繞著恒星轉，恒星繞著更大的恒星轉，這樣繼續下去一直到達星系的中心。我們看似淩亂的星空，其實早已是宇宙設定好的"運行方式"。

Planets revolve around stars, and stars revolve around bigger stars, and so on until they reach the center of galaxies. Our seemingly messy starry sky has long been a "running mode" set by the universe.

每個人"轉世輪回"的模式和行星恒星的"運行方式"相似，也同樣是已經設定好的。

The pattern of each person's "reincarnation" is similar to the "running mode "of planets and stars, and is also already set.

一個人看似隨機的生活，但所謂的"人生大事"，也早就已經安排好了 [1]（這就是為什麼古人會說"一切皆有定數"）。

A person's life may seem random, but the so-called "major events in life" have already been arranged [1] (this is why the ancients said "everything is predetermined").

因為在轉世前，你已經簡單地預覽過你的一生。看到這句話，相信每個人都會很難理解。在此舉個例子，你簡單地預覽了你試卷上的題目，但題目的答案需要你自己來填寫。[2]

Because before reincarnation, you have already simply glanced over your life. Seeing this sentence, I believe everyone will find it difficult to understand. Here is an example, you simply glanced over the questions on your test paper, but you need to fill in the answers to the questions yourself. [2]

而且你會遇到怎樣的家庭、工作、伴侶也都是有原因的：第一，是為了你靈魂進化的"任務"；第二，也在於你前些世都做了些什麼。你之所以會成為現在這個"你"，跟前些世"犯過的錯"和"努過的力"都有關 [3]。

Furthermore, there are reasons for the family, job, and partner you encounter: first, it is for the "mission" of your soul's evolution; second, it is also due to what you did in previous lives. The reason why you are who you are now is related to the "mistakes you made" and "efforts you made" in previous lives [3].

比如：一個人總感覺自己周邊的人缺點很多，那麼你就要先審視一下自己是否也存在著這些缺點。而這一世你為什麼會跟他們在一起，是有原因的。也許前些世的你，就有過類似的缺點，或犯過同樣的錯誤。所以，只有認清自己，才能夠修對方向。

For instance: If a person always feels that the people around him have many shortcomings, then you should first examine whether you yourself also possess these shortcomings. And there is a reason why you are in this world with them. Maybe in a previous life, you had similar shortcomings or made the same mistakes. Therefore, only by recognizing yourself can you cultivate in the right direction.

還有如果人生中遇到了某些困難，請記住不要抱怨任何人，因為這都是你要面對的考驗，也是自己"本世選好的課題"[4]。

Also, if you encounter certain difficulties in life, please remember not to complain to anyone, because these are the tests you have to face and the "lessons you have chosen for this life" [4].

你要記住，在靈魂進化的過程中"不在於你這一生是什麼樣的人，而在於你這一世都做了些什麼[5]"。

You must remember that in the process of soul evolution, "it is not about who you are in this life, but what you do in this life [5]".

注 Note

[1] 命運雖然安排好了一些內容，但很多事情都可以往好的方向修改，因為人都有自由的意志。但記住不要嘗試用"算命"的方式去修改自己的命運，轉世後知道未來會發生什麼是有違自然的，在"高級自我"看來你等於通過某些手段去洩露"試卷的題目"。所以請選擇順隨自然，勇敢地去面對未來的生活，"高我"會喜歡幫助誠實勇敢的人。

Although fate has arranged some things, many things can be modified for the better, because people have free will. But remember not to try to modify your own fate by "fortune-telling". It is against nature to know what will happen in the future after reincarnation. In the eyes of the "higher self", you are equivalent to leaking the "questions on the test paper" through some means. So please choose to follow nature and face the future life bravely. The "higher self" will like to help honest and brave people.

[2] 每個人轉世前，都會在"高級自我"那裡預覽下一世生活的"簡短片段"，而這些生活中的片段，正是你下一世要所面對的"課題"，至於這些課題能不能做好，就看你靈性的發揮了。

Before reincarnation, everyone will view "brief fragments" of their next life in the "higher self", and these fragments of life are exactly the "lessons" you will face in your next life. As for whether you can do well in these lessons, it depends on your spiritual development.

[3] 由於"因果業力"的原因，你對別人做過的任何事情，不管是"好的事情還是壞的事情"，都會在未來的某個時間，以不同的方式體驗到自己的身上。

Due to the law of cause and effect, anything you do to others, whether it is "good or bad", will be experienced by you in different ways at some time in the future.

[4] 就算當世的生活再難，也絕不可以提前結束自己當世的物理生命，切記！不然下一世還會繼續過完上一世沒有過完的生活，經歷更難的考驗。

而且有些人一直困惑，難道那些犯罪的人，命運也是選好的嗎？

在此要說明的是：轉世前雖然大部分的命運"課題"是自己選好的，但填寫"課題的答案"時有些人可能會填錯，因為人都有自由的意志。

No matter how difficult life is in this world, you must never end your physical life in advance, remember! Otherwise, you will continue to live the unfinished life in the next life and experience more difficult tests.

Some people have always been confused, do those who commit crimes also have their fates chosen? Here I want to explain that although most of the fate "questions" are chosen by oneself before reincarnation, some people may fill in the "answers to the questions" incorrectly because people have free will.

[5] 每個人每世的生活都是為了要讓自己學到更多，也是為了要讓自己的靈魂進化程度更高。而在靈魂進化的過程中，不在於你當世是什麼樣的"身份或地位"，而在於你在這個"角色"都學到了什麼，做了什麼。具體知識點可查閱《海奧華預言》第十章。

[5] Everyone lives in every life to learn more and to make their soul evolve to a higher level. In the process of soul evolution, it does not matter what your "identity or status" is in this life, but what you have learned and done in this "role". For specific knowledge points, please refer to Chapter 10 of "Thiaoouba Prophecy".

40

那些善良優秀的人，請一定要明白這個道理
Those kind and excellent people, please be sure to understand this truth.

善良優秀的人（也就是靈性較高的人），經常會有莫名的孤獨感，這是正常的。

Kind and excellent people (that is, people with higher spirituality) often have an inexplicable sense of loneliness, which is normal.

因為在轉世前，你靈魂的進化程度就已有相當高的水準 [1]，在轉到本世時，學習那些該學習的知識會顯得毫不費力，也很快可以在人群中做到出類拔萃。

Because your soul had already evolved to a very high level before your reincarnation [1]. When you reincarnate into this life, it will be effortless for you to learn the knowledge you need to learn, and you will soon be able to stand out from the crowd.

然而某些靈魂淨化程度稍低的人，對這種善良優秀的人，難免會產生妒忌、憎恨或者是排斥 [2]。

However, some people whose souls are less purified will inevitably feel jealousy, hatred, or rejection towards such kind and excellent people [2].

這也是為什麼在你沒招惹某些人的情況下，某些人有時會看你不順眼的原因。

This is also the reason why some people may sometimes dislike you even if you don't provoke them.

所以請不要因為這種"孤獨感"，而感到困惑。當你明白這個道理時，你的那些孤獨感將會逐漸地消失。

So please don't be confused by this "loneliness". When you understand this truth, your loneliness will gradually disappear.

如果你是那個善良優秀的人，請不要太在意別人的看法。繼續做好你該做的事，問心無愧的事，多做那些有意義的事，幫助需要幫助的人 [3]。

If you are a kind and excellent person, please do not care too much about what others think. Continue to do what you should do, do things with a clear conscience, do more meaningful things, and help those in need [3].

這樣一來，那些靈魂淨化程度稍低的人們，就會由妒忌和憎恨，轉化為對你的尊重和學習。

In this way, those whose souls are less purified will change their jealousy and hatred into respect and learning from you.

注 Note

[1] "就像那些很年輕就被稱為天才的人那樣——仿佛他們早已成竹在胸。"此句出自《海奧華預言》第十一章。很多人擁有的"天賦"，基本是"前些世"積累下來的知識和經驗。

"Like the very young people now on Earth, who are called geniuses because they seem to have a calculation in their heads" This sentence comes from chapter 11 of "Thiaoouba prophecy".The "talents" that many people possess are basically the knowledge and experience accumulated from "previous lives".

[2] "妒忌和仇恨僅有一步之差。"此句出自《海奧華預言》第三章。而且一個人在靈魂進化的修行過程中，"妒忌"是最應該先戒掉的壞習慣，因為它會真正阻礙你"個人靈性"的發展。修行中要用"我能學到些什麼？又能分享些什麼？"這樣的心態去修行，而不能用跟別人"對比高低"的心態去修行。如果一個人總想著跟別人去比"高低"，那麼這個人就會產生更多的攻擊心和妒忌心，從而不利於他個人靈性的發展。

"there is only one step from envy to hate "This sentence comes from the third chapter of "Thiaoouba Prophecy". Moreover, in the process of spiritual evolution, "jealousy" is the bad habit that should be abandoned first, because it will really hinder the development of your "personal spirituality". In spiritual practice, you should practice with the mentality of "what can I learn? What can I share?" instead of practicing with the mentality of "comparing with others". If a person always thinks of "comparing with others", then this person will have more aggressiveness and jealousy, which is not conducive to his personal spiritual development.

[3] "解決問題的辦法取決於愛，不是錢，這需要人們超越仇恨、厭

惡、憤怒和猜忌。並且每個人，無論他是街道清潔人員還是社區領袖，都將身邊的人放在自己之前，對任何需要幫助的人都施以援手。"具體信息可查閱《海奧華預言》第九章。

"the solution depends on love - not money. It requires that people rise above hate, resentment, jealousy and envy, and that each person, whether he be street sweeper or community leader, put his neighbour before himself, offering his hand to whoever needs it. "For detailed information, please refer to Chapter 9 of the "Thiaoouba Prophecy".

41

是否選擇"靈魂進化程度"的提升，是自己決定的
Whether to choose to improve the "degree of soul evolution" is up to you

你的能力，你的優勢，你的福報，這一切基本都是前些世累積修來的。

Your abilities, your advantages, your blessings, all of these are basically the accumulation of your past lives.

然而一個人在每世的靈魂進化修行過程中，有"提升"的時候，也會有"下降"的時候。

However, in the process of a person's soul evolution in each life, there are times of "ascension" and times of "descent".

舉個例子：如果你現在是某個"有能力或者有權力"的人，不能因為你有能力或有權利，就去欺騙他人，就去墮落腐敗，就去做一些違反自然法則的事情。

For example, if you are a "capable or powerful person" now, you can't deceive others, go corrupt and do something that violates the laws of nature just because you are capable or powerful.

如果這樣做的話，你的"靈魂進化程度"就會因此受到影響，在整個"生命輪回體系"中，這一世就會產生"負加分"，從而拖累你靈魂進化的進度。

If you do this, your "degree of soul evolution" will be affected. In the entire "reincarnation system", this life will generate "negative points", thus slowing down the progress of your soul evolution.

相反，如果這一世，你做了很多正直、善良 [1]、有意義的事情，也發現了自己很多的缺點，並在這世生活中努力改正了。

On the contrary, if in this life you have done many upright, kind [1] and meaningful things, and also discovered many of your own shortcomings, and worked hard to correct them in this life.

那麼你這一世，就會對"整個生命輪回體系"做出很大的貢獻，靈魂進化程度上將會獲得較高的提升，前進的步伐也會更快。

Then, in this life, you will make a great contribution to the "entire life reincarnation system", the degree of soul evolution will be greatly improved, and the pace of progress will be faster.

要記住，無論如何都不能因"目前這世"受到的不良影響，而造成"靈魂進化"上的退步。在每一世靈魂進化的過程中，"不在於你這一生是什麼樣的人，而在於你這一生都做了些什麼。"

Remember, no matter what, you must not let the negative effects of your current life cause you to regress in your "soul evolution." In the process of soul evolution in each life, "it's not about who you are in this life, but what you have done in this life."

注 Note

[1] 每個人都喜歡與正直善良的人交朋友，與正直善良的人共事，尊敬正直善良的人，因為這是人類的天性和靈魂所向。雖然有些人受當前社會的影響，为了利益表面上結交了一些狡詐的人，但他們的內心裡也一定是排斥的。

Everyone likes to make friends with honest and kind people, work with honest and kind people, and respect honest and kind people, because this is human nature and soul yearning. Although some people are influenced by the current society and make friends with some cunning people for the sake of profit on the surface, they must be rejecting them in their hearts.

42

生活中的每一個課題，都是在為以後的"任務"做鋪墊
Every lesson in life is paving the way for future "tasks"

一個人在生活中遇到的所有事情，基本是在進行著他本世要做的"課題"。

Everything that a person encounters in life is basically the "lessons" that he will encounter in this life.

人的一生其實是自己"選擇好的"[1]，來這一世就是為了要鍛煉自己的"靈性"。你出生的家庭、接觸過的工作、遇到的眾人，也基本是有原因的，所以你要努力明白自己"前來"本世的目的。

A person's life is actually "chosen" by himself [1]. The purpose of coming to this life is to cultivate one's "spirituality". The family you were born into, the jobs you have been involved in, and the people you have met all have reasons, so you must work hard to understand the purpose of your "coming" to this life.

"就是說，你所遇到的每一件事情，都基本是在為以後的任務做鋪墊，也是在為靈魂進化上的進步做鍛煉。"

"That is to say, everything you encounter is basically paving the way for future tasks and training for your soul's progress in evolution."

而且每個人每世的"課題"都是獨立的存在 [2]，所以一定不要羨慕或鄙視別人的生活，更沒必要讓自己"活"得像誰 [3]，你只需要記住不斷地進步自己和修掉自己的缺點就可以。

Moreover, each person's "lessons" in each life exist independently [2], so you must not envy or despise other people's lives, and there is no need to make yourself "live" like someone else [3]. You just need to remember to constantly improve yourself and correct your own shortcomings.

還有，一個人如果想要獲得"更高級的知識"，首先你必須要在某些基本領域得到提升 [4]。因為只有充分瞭解了基本知識，才能對未來遇到的"高級知識"，更容易地吸收和理解。

Furthermore, if a person wants to acquire "more advanced knowledge", he must first improve in certain basic areas [4]. This is because only by fully understanding the basic knowledge can one more easily absorb and understand the "advanced knowledge" that one encounters in the future.

比如，一個 1 年級的學生，突然獲得了一本 5 年級的考題答案，他是不會理解的，他只有把 2、3、4 年級的知識學習充分，才能理解這本答案是如此的珍貴 [5]。

For example, if a first-grade student suddenly gets a book of answers to fifth-grade test questions, he will not understand what is going on. Only after he has fully learned the knowledge from second, third, and fourth grades can he understand how valuable this book of answers is [5].

注 Note

[1] 每個人轉世前，都會在"高級自我"那裡預覽下一世生活的"簡短片段"，而這些生活中的片段，正是你下一世要所面對的"課題"，至於這些課題能不能做好，就看你靈性的發揮了。

Before reincarnation, everyone will view "brief fragments" of their next life in the "higher self", and these fragments of life are exactly the "lessons" you will face in your next life. As for whether you can do well in these lessons, it depends on your spiritual development.

[2] 比如全球有 70 億人口，這 70 億人中沒有一個人與另一個人的指紋是相同的，也沒有一個人與另一個人的命運是相同的，每一個人都是獨立的存在。

For example, there are 7 billion people in the world. Among these 7 billion people, no one has the same fingerprint as another, and no one has the same destiny as another. Every person is an independent existence.

[3] 你沒必要羨慕那些所謂的"成功人士"，更沒必要去模仿他們的生活方式去追求自己的生活。其實，我們每一個人都可以比作是"金子"做的，俗話說是金子總會發光，如果你感覺自己的那個"金身"還沒有"發光"，無非就是金身"表層的泥土和污垢沒有清理乾淨罷了"，所以請努力發現自己的缺點修掉它。

You don't need to envy those so-called "successful people", and you don't need to imitate their lifestyle. In fact, each of us can be compared to being made of "gold". As the saying goes, gold always shines. If you feel that your "golden body" has not "shine" yet, it is nothing more than "the dirt and grime on the surface of the golden body has not been cleaned up", so please work hard to find your own shortcomings and fix them.

[4] 無論是佛學，還是道家、基督教等宗教裡面都在傳遞著一些相似的知識點，比如：人有靈魂，轉世輪回，因果業力，順隨自然，要有愛心，等等。這些相似的知識點一定不是所謂的迷信，而是從那些遙遠的年代傳承下來的真理。我們可以綜合起來去瞭解這些相似的知識點，而不能對某個教派產生盲目崇拜。一個人一旦產生了盲目崇拜，那麼他就不會再去專注自己內心的修行，而是去專注那些被他崇拜的人或事物。這也是佛陀反對個人崇拜的原因。

Whether it is Buddhism, Taoism, Christianity or other religions, they all convey some similar knowledge points, such as: people have souls, reincarnation, cause and effect, follow nature, have love, etc. These similar knowledge points are definitely not so-called superstitions, but truths passed down from those distant times. We can understand these similar knowledge points in a comprehensive way, and we should not blindly worship a certain sect. Once a person has blind worship, he will no longer focus on his own inner practice, but on the people or things he worships. This is also the reason why Buddha opposes the cult of personality.

[5] 前幾篇短文總提到的《海奧華預言》這本書，請相信我這本書絕對不是一本科幻小說，而是幾乎涵蓋了佛學、道家、聖經裡最核心的知識在裡面，如果你能換一種思維把這本書耐心地連讀數遍，那麼你將會瞭解更多你想知道的秘密。

The book "Thiaoouba prophecy" mentioned in the previous short articles, please believe me, this book is definitely not a science fiction novel, but it covers almost the most core knowledge of Buddhism, Taoism, and the Bible. If you can change your mindset and patiently read this book several times, then you will understand more secrets you want to know.

43

什麼是"靈性"上的鍛煉？
What is spiritual exercise?

很多人不明白什麼是靈性上的鍛煉。其實"靈性上的鍛煉"跟"體育上的鍛煉"非常相似。

Many people do not understand what spiritual exercise is. In fact, "spiritual exercise" is very similar to "physical exercise".

舉個例子，一個普通人，如果他想變成一名長跑運動員，首先，他一定要突破跑 5 公里的難度，然後再突破 10 公里的，只有經過持續的鍛煉，他才能變成一名長跑運動員。

For example, if an ordinary person wants to become a long-distance runner, first, he must break through the difficulty of running 5 kilometers, and then break through 10 kilometers. Only through continuous training can he become a long-distance runner.

一名登山者，如果他想要登上"珠峰"，那麼他一定要先去攀登一些"常規高度的山峰"，只有經過持續地增加鍛煉和吸取經驗，他最後才能登上世界上"最高的山峰"。

If a mountaineer wants to climb Mount Everest, he must first climb some "mountains of regular height". Only after continuous training and gaining experience can he finally climb the "highest mountain" in the world.

而靈性上的鍛煉，跟上邊舉的這兩個例子基本相同。

The spiritual exercise is basically the same as the two examples given above.

如果你想獲得更高的靈性，首先你必須接受眾多事物的考驗，在人生中經歷各種各樣的體驗才行。有時，你也需要完成一些"更有難度"的事情 [1]，這樣你的靈性才能得到更充分地鍛煉。

If you want to achieve a higher spirituality, you must first be tested by many things and experience a variety of experiences in life. Sometimes, you also need to complete some "more difficult" things [1] so that your spirituality can be more fully exercised.

實際上，在你當下的生活中就包含著本世要鍛煉的"課題"，隨著生活中"課題"的處理能力越來越強和完善，你的"靈性"就會在某些階段中得到相應的提升。

In fact, your current life contains the "lessons" that you need to learn in this life. As your ability to handle the "lessons" in your life becomes stronger and more complete, your "spirituality" will be improved accordingly at certain stages.

而且，提升靈性是一個循序漸進的過程，我們都需要一點一點地鍛煉，不能一心只想著看幾遍"靈性書籍"，就迫切地想要獲得"超越常人的能力"，我們也不能太著急。

Moreover, improving spirituality is a gradual process. We all need to practice little by little. We cannot just think about reading "spiritual books" a few times and eagerly want to gain "abilities beyond ordinary people". We cannot be too anxious.

古人用"修"這個字，是有道理的。你要明白，正常出生在初級星球上的我們 [2]，註定是不完美的，所以我們要不斷地修正自己的心態，修正自己的行為，發現自己的缺點，認清自己才行。

There is a reason why the Chinese ancients used the word "（修）cultivation". You have to understand that we who are born on the first category of planets [2] are destined to be imperfect, so we must constantly correct our mindset, correct our behavior, discover our shortcomings, and recognize ourselves.

當一個人的心理心態、思想行為，都進入了一個正確的運行方式，堅持按照正確的知識方向走，時間久了"高級自我"就會向你傳遞更多意想不到的知識 [3]。

When a person's psychological state of mind, thoughts and behaviors have entered a correct mode of operation and he insists on following the correct direction of knowledge, over time the "higher self" will pass on more unexpected knowledge to you [3].

"神助自助者"，顯然我們做的每一件事，"高級自我"都在觀察著我們。

"God helps those who help themselves." Apparently, everything we do is being watched by our higher selves.

注 Note

[1] 有些靈魂在選擇轉世的時候，有時會故意選擇到一個"比較艱難"的環境中去生活，因為他感覺這樣可以使自己的靈性得到更充分的鍛煉。比如你準備要去幫助一群受苦受難的人，如果你不把自己置身在他們的生活中待一段時間，去體會一下他們的感受，那麼你將永遠不會知道，他們真正需要幫助的地方是什麼。

而在幫助自己靈魂的修行中也是一樣，如果你想快速提升自己的靈性，那麼你就需要完成一些比較"特殊的課題"，因為有時候不經歷一些特殊的課題，你可能永遠不會知道，你需要提升的地方在哪裡。而這種"特殊的課題"也往往存在於某些較為艱難的生活場景中。

通過這些生活中的場景，你充分鍛煉了自己的靈性，修掉了自己的缺點，幫助了自己的靈魂，提升了自己的靈性。

所以說"高級自我"與你一起精心選擇的每一世都很重要，都是為了你靈魂進化的提升"量身定做的"。

但無論當世遇到的"事情再難"，也都不能提前放棄自己當世的物理生命，不然下一世還會繼續過完前一世未過完的生活，經歷同樣類型更難的考驗。

When some souls choose to reincarnate, they sometimes deliberately choose to live in a "more difficult" environment, because they feel that this will allow their spirituality to be more fully exercised. For example, if you are going to help a group of suffering people, if you do not put yourself in their lives for a period of time to experience their feelings, then you will never know what they really need help with.

The same is true in helping your own soul. If you want to quickly improve your spirituality, you need to complete some "special lessons". Sometimes, without going through some special lessons, you may never know where you need to improve. And this kind of "special lesson" often exists in some difficult life scenarios.

Through these scenes in life, you have fully exercised your spirituality, corrected your shortcomings, helped your soul, and improved your spirituality.

Therefore, every life that your "higher self" carefully chooses with you is very important and is "tailor-made" for the improvement of your soul's evolution.

But no matter how difficult things are in this life, you cannot give up your physical life in advance, otherwise you will continue to live the unfinished life in the previous life in the next life, and experience the same type of more difficult tests.

[2] 地球就是一個初級修煉場，這裡有非常特殊的教學環境。也就是說正常出生在地球上的人類，都要從比較艱難的生活方式開始鍛煉，只有經過充分的鍛煉，使精神層面上能夠得到提升，未來才能進入更高級的生活環境。具體知識點可查閱《海奧華預言》第六章，有詳細描述。

The Earth is a primary training ground, with a very special teaching environment. That is to say, humans born on Earth must start training from a relatively difficult lifestyle. Only after sufficient training can the spiritual level be improved and they can enter a more advanced living environment in the future. Specific knowledge points can be found in the sixth chapter of "Thiaoouba Prophecy", which is described in detail.

[3] 古人所說的"頭上三尺有神靈"其實就是你的"高級自我"，你做的每一件事都會被"高級自我"記錄下來。而且"神助自助者"也是真實存在的，你的努力，你的付出，你的德行，也一直

被觀察著，"高級自我"會時不時地給你些推動。還有我們雙手交合做出的祈禱和許願，也都是我們自己的"高級自我"幫助我們實現的，而"高我"只會時不時地滿足我們的"正確願望"。當然你也不能總是依賴高我的幫助，你需要自己付出行動和努力，"高我"最喜歡幫助"努力向上"的人。

What the ancients said about "there are gods above your head" is actually your "higher self". Everything you do will be recorded by the "higher self". Moreover, "God helps those who help themselves" is real. Your efforts, your contributions, and your virtues are also being observed. The "higher self" will give you some push from time to time. In addition, the prayers and wishes we make with our hands together are also realized by our own "higher self". The "higher self" will only satisfy our "correct wishes" from time to time. Of course, you can't always rely on the help of the higher self. You need to take action and work hard on your own. The "higher self" likes to help those who "work hard to move forward" the most.

44

如何看待一個人"靈性"的高低?
又該如何提高自己的"靈性"?
How to judge a person's "spirituality"?
How to improve your own spirituality?

如何看待一個人"靈性"的高低？在現實生活中，如果一個人的靈性很高，相應地，這個人在生活中的能力也會表現得很高。

How do we judge the level of a person's "spirituality"? In real life, if a person's spirituality is high, then correspondingly, this person's ability in life will also be high.

可如果一個人的"能力"很高，卻不能代表著這個人的"靈性"就高，這是為什麼？

But if a person's "ability" is high, it does not mean this person's "spirituality" is high. Why?

舉個例子：那些設計危險武器或製造有害科技的人們，他們的能力和智商都很高，但由於靈魂淨化程度的問題，他們把能力和智商用錯了方向，那麼這些"高能力高智商"的人們，他們的靈性相比其他善良的人來說，卻是很低的。

For example: Those who design dangerous weapons or create harmful technologies have high abilities and IQs, but due to the problem of the degree of soul purification, they use their abilities and IQs in the wrong direction. Therefore, these "highly capable and highly intelligent" people have very low spirituality compared to other kind people.

事實上，一個人的"靈性"中包含了很多內容，比如：愛心、友善、感恩、謙遜、真誠、和諧、喜悅、靈敏、勇敢、正直、光明、公正、平和、自律、自由、尊敬、仁慈、大度、寬容、毅力、定力、恒心、創造性、優雅、智慧，等等，"靈性"中包含一個人很多方面的優點。

In fact, a person's "spirituality" includes many things, such as love, kindness, gratitude, humility, sincerity, harmony, joy, sensitivity, courage, integrity, positive, fairness, peace, self-discipline, freedom, respect, mercy, generosity, tolerance, perseverance, concentration, persistence, creativity, elegance, wisdom, etc. "Spirituality" includes many aspects of a person's merits.

一個人只有把這些優點"綜合"起來看，才能判斷這個人靈性的高低。

Only by "combining" these merits can one judge the spiritual level of a person.

然而一個人如果想要提升自己的"靈性"，就要努力從各個方面找到自己不足的地方，進行自我"修正"[1]。只有把自己各個方面的優點均衡地提升，才能使自己的"靈性"得到有效地提升。

However, if a person wants to improve his "spirituality", he must try to find his own shortcomings in all aspects and make self-correction[1].

Only by improving the advantages of all aspects in a balanced way can we effectively improve our spirituality.

當然，靈性的提升，更有助於"靈魂的進化"，這會讓一個人在"整個輪回體系"中進步得更快。

Of course, spiritual improvement helps the "evolution of the soul," which allows a person to progress faster in the "entire reincarnation system."

注 Note

[1] 我們不斷地"修行"，其實就是為了提高自己的靈性。在當下的生活中就包含著本世要修行的"課題"，只要把遇到的所有課題都儘量按正面的方式去處理完善，那麼靈性就會在"生活課題的鍛煉"中得到提升。而靈性中最重要的一點就是愛心，如果一個人的愛心程度跟不上，靈性就會提升得很慢，還有可能會下降。所以如果想要提高自己的靈性，首先要做的就是提高自己的愛心。

We are constantly "practicing" to improve our spirituality. In our current life, there are "lessons" to learn. As long as we try to deal with and improve all the issues we encounter in a positive way, our spirituality will be improved in the "training of life issues". The most important thing in spirituality is love. If a person's love level cannot keep up, his spirituality will improve very slowly and may even decline. So if you want to improve your spirituality, the first thing you need to do is to improve your love.

45

"精神"和"靈魂"的關係是什麼？
What is the relationship between spirit(psyche) and soul(Astral body)?

請記住：人的一生，所有物質都是暫時為你服務的"工具"，能獲得精神上的體驗才是最終目的。因為在輪迴時 [1]，只有你的精神和靈魂會被帶走 [2]。

Remember this: Throughout one's life, all material things are merely "tools" serving you temporarily. The ultimate goal is to gain spiritual experiences. Because when you reincarnate [1], only your spirit and soul will be taken away [2].

那精神和靈魂的關係到底是什麼？

What is the relationship between spirit(psyche) and soul (Astral body)?

靈魂是精神的載體，靈魂是由電子組成 [3]，我們可以把它看作一個實體，而精神是靈魂的一部分。舉個通俗易懂的例子："靈魂"我們可以把它比作成"硬件"，而"精神"則可以比作成"軟件"。轉世時，"記憶數據"雖然被表面地清除了，但靈魂中儲存的"經

驗和方法 ”會有所保留。

The soul is the carrier of the spirit. The soul is composed of electrons [3]. We can regard it as an entity, and the spirit is a part of the soul. To give an easy-to-understand example, we can compare the "soul" to "hardware" and the "spirit" to "software". When reincarnated, although the "memory data" is superficially cleared, the "experience and methods" stored in the soul will be retained.

也就是說，雖然你表面忘記了前些世所有的事情 [4]，但那些精神上的高度和靈魂進化上的優點，會得以保留 [5]，這會使你的下一世進步得更快，你自身的天賦優勢也會更加明顯。

In other words, although you may seem to have forgotten everything from your previous lives[4], your spiritual achievements and advantages in soul evolution will be retained[5], which will enable you to progress faster in your next life, and your own innate advantages will become more obvious.

還有，我們每個人都有著 “同樣 ” 的靈魂，每個靈魂都擁有 40 萬億億個電子，但每個人在 “處理事情的能力 ” 和 “對待事物的價值觀 ” 上，卻存在著很大的差距，出現這種情況的原因在於，人與人之間的精神進化程度和修為有所不同。

In addition, each of us has the same soul(Astral body), and each soul has 4 billion trillion electrons, but each person has a huge gap in "ability to handle things" and "values towards things". The reason for this is that the degree of spiritual evolution and cultivation of people are different.

注 Note

[1] 關於輪迴的知識，在古印度寺廟中的 Naacal 石板上是這樣記載的：“人的靈魂將會再次存在。永恆不朽的靈魂就彷彿是一個神聖的火花，在這個火花的基礎上，用各種元素組成了一個身體將其包裹起來，就跟一個房子一樣。這個房子是由基本的細胞組成的，並由生命力量聚集和連接。在經過慣常的一個週期之後，這種基本化合物就會耗盡，並返回大地，於此同時也就釋放了該神聖的火花。在一個特定的時間，一組新的基本細胞就會被聚集在一起，一個新的房子被再次建造，包裹着神聖的火花。作爲基本的細胞，這個房子也會重新回到大地，再次釋放神聖的火花。這個過程就這樣繼續下去，神聖的花不斷地佔據一個又一個的房子，直到最終被召喚回到它來的地方——神聖源頭（Divine Source）此段內容出自《The children of Mu》。

而且就算知道了靈魂是永生的，我們也要珍惜當下的每一世生活，不能期盼着“早日輪迴”。每個人每世需要完成的“課題”都是獨立的，不要羨慕或鄙視任何人，不需要跟任何人比，但你要學會認可自己，改正自己，平穩自己，進步自己。

不管一個人處在什麼樣的生活環境，出生在什麼樣的家庭，目前是什麼樣的身份，都要認真對待當下的這一世，不可頹廢。

The knowledge about reincarnation is recorded on the Naacal slate in ancient Indian temples:"It is the man, the spirit, which comes into being again. Imperishable man is a Divine Spark upon which a house or an encasing body is built out of elements. This encasing house is com menced by elementary cells being formed and brought together and joined by the ziis of the Life Force. After the usual period, this elementary compound wears out and returns to Mother Earth, thus setting the Divine Spark free. At the appointed time a new set of elemen tary cells is brought together and a new house is built again, encasing the Divine Spark. Being elementary, this house also returns to Mother Earth, again releasing and setting the Divine Spark free. And so it continues, the Divine Spark occupying one house after another until called, it then returns whence it came. The Divine Source."This passage is from The children of Mu.

Even if we know that the soul is immortal, we should cherish every life we have now and not look forward to "reincarnation soon". Everyone has their own "tasks" to complete in each life. Don't envy or despise anyone, and don't compare yourself with anyone, but you must learn to recognize yourself, correct yourself, stabilize yourself, and improve yourself.

No matter what kind of living environment a person is in, what kind of family he is born into, or what his current identity is, he must take the present life seriously and not be decadent.

[2] 現在伸出你的雙手，看著它，仔細想一想，在這個世界中有什麼物質會是真正屬於你的？就連我們的身體，也只是暫時屬於我們自己。我們來到這個世界上的目的，就是為了來獲得精神體驗的，因為只有我們的精神和靈魂才是真正屬於我們自己。所以，不要執著於物質主義的生活，因為所有的物質只是暫時為你服務的工具。

Now reach out your hands, look at them, and think carefully. What material things in this world can truly belong to you? Even our bodies only belong to us temporarily. The purpose of our coming to this world is to gain spiritual experience, because only our spirit and soul truly belong to ourselves. Therefore, do not cling to a materialistic life, because all materials are just tools to serve you temporarily.

[3] "無論如何，你的肉體都將損壞並終有死亡的那一天。而你的精

神，作為靈體的一部分，永不消亡。"此句出自《海奧華預言》第六章。

"一個正常人類的靈體大約是由四十萬億億個電子組成，它整好與你的物理外形相匹配。"具體內容請查閱《海奧華預言》第十三章，有詳細描述。

"but, regardless, your physical body will wear out and die one day, whereas your psyche, being part of your Astral body, never dies. "This sentence comes from the sixth chapter of the "Thiaoouba Prophecy".

"A normal human Astral body is composed of about 4 billion trillion electrons, exactly marrying your physical shape. "For details, please refer to chapter 13 of "Thiaoouba Prophecy", which is described in detail.

[4] 舉例是為了讓讀者能夠大致理解靈魂和精神之間的關係，實際上二者之間的關係要遠比此文描述的例子複雜得多。

而且很多人困惑為什麼轉世時要"清除記憶"，而清除記憶對我們來說，應該看作是造物主給我們的一種恩惠，如果人的每一世都能想起前世的事情，那在過當下的生活時一定會很無趣，也不會感到驚喜。

還有就像《海奧華預言》的作者米歇有一世喝多了做了蠢事的那次，如果他本世一開始就知道前世做過不該做的事情，那麼他本世一定會帶著愧疚去度過此生，所以，應該把清除記憶看作是一種恩惠。

[4] The examples given are intended to help readers understand the relationship between soul and spirit. In fact, the relationship between the two is far more complicated than the examples described in this article.

Many people are also confused about why they need to "erase their memories" when they reincarnate. However, for us, erasing our memories should be seen as a blessing from the Creator. If people could remember things from their previous lives in every life, then their present life would be very boring and they would not feel any surprises.

Also, like the time when Michel Desmarquet, the author of "Thiaoouba Prophecy", got drunk and did something stupid in one of his lives, if he had known from the beginning that he had done something he shouldn't have done in his previous life, he would have spent this life with guilt. Therefore, erasing memory should be seen as a blessing.

[5] 轉世的時候，精神會得以保留，而精神又分為正面精神和負面精神，正面精神就是我們所說的靈性，靈性中包含了"愛心、友善、感恩、謙遜、真誠、和諧、喜悅、靈敏、勇敢、正直、光明、公正、平和、自律、自由、尊敬、仁慈、大度、寬容、毅力、定力、恒心、創造性、優雅、智慧，等等"，而與之相反的就可以看作是負面精神，正面精神和負面精神都是從累世的生活中建立到靈魂上的，這些精神都會在轉世的時候，跟著靈魂去到下一世。修行中修的是什麼？就是要把負面精神修掉，讓自己的正面精神（靈性）更高，這樣我們的靈魂進化程度就會越來越高。

When reincarnation occurs, the spirit is preserved. The spirit can be divided into positive and negative aspects. The positive aspect of the spirit is what we call spirituality. Spirituality includes qualities such as love, kindness, gratitude, humility, sincerity, harmony, joy, sensitivity, courage, integrity, brightness, fairness, peace, self-discipline, freedom, respect, compassion, generosity, tolerance, perseverance, determination, consistency, creativity, grace, and wisdom, among others.

In contrast, the opposite qualities can be seen as negative aspects of the spirit. Both positive and negative spirits are imprinted onto the soul through countless lifetimes of experience, and they accompany the soul into the next life during reincarnation.

What is the purpose of spiritual practice? It is to remove the negative aspects of the spirit and to elevate the positive ones—our spirituality—so that our soul may evolve to a higher level.

46

我們為什麼會生存在"二元一體"的世界裡
Why do we live in a world of "duality"

有黑色才能體現出白色的白，有寒冷才能感受到炎熱的熱。這世界的一切基本是"二元一體"的存在，是非常合理的設計，因為只有這樣，才能讓我們感受到更多精神上的體驗。

Only black can reflect white, and only cold can feel heat. Everything in this world is basically a "duality "existence, which is a very reasonable design, because only in this way can we feel more spiritual experience.

比如，前面有座高山，當你爬到山頂時，你會看到一望無際的風景，感到"非常美麗"，你也會看到萬丈深淵的懸崖，從而"心生恐懼"；或許你可能會想"為什麼會有這麼深的懸崖？這麼危險，我要掉下去怎麼辦？"

For example, there is a high mountain ahead. When you climb to the top, you will see the endless scenery and feel "very beautiful". You will also see the cliff with a bottomless abyss and feel "fear". Or you may think, "Why is there such a deep cliff? It is so dangerous. What if I fall down?"

那你有沒有想過，如果沒有這個"懸崖"，也就沒有這座"高山"，那你體驗到的將是一個"平地"。

Have you ever thought that if there was no "cliff", there would be no "mountain", and what you would experience would be a "flat land".

再舉個例子，天氣正熱的夏天，有一個人正在山路間行走（沒有帶水），行走了一段山路之後，他感覺自己非常口渴，就這樣走著走著，他發現一塊大石頭的下方正在不斷地湧出"泉水"，這時他捧起山泉暢飲，感覺到泉水是如此的"甘甜"。

To give another example, on a hot summer day, a man was walking on a mountain road (without bringing water). After walking for a while, he felt very thirsty. As he walked, he found that "spring water" was constantly gushing out from under a large rock. At this time, he scooped up the spring water and drank it, feeling that the spring water was so "sweet".

那你有沒有想過，如果這個人沒經歷過"口渴"，他怎能深刻感受到這泉水的"甘甜"？

Then have you ever thought about this: if this person has never experienced "thirst", how can he deeply feel the "sweetness" of the spring water?

舉的這兩個例子是為了讓大家明白，我們生存在二元一體的世界裡，目的就是為了要尋求到更多精神上的的體驗 [1]。而你目前在地球上經歷的一切，也是為了以後去更高等的星球，體驗到更好的感覺，而作下的鋪墊 [2]。

The purpose of these two examples is to make everyone understand that we live in a dualistic world in order to seek more spiritual experiences [1]. And everything you are experiencing on Earth now is also a preparation for going to a higher planet in the future and experiencing better feelings [2].

如果你懂得了這個道理，那麼你就會理解《海奧華預言》書中說過的那段：“你在你的星球上是為了學習如何生存，經歷苦難，和麵對死亡，以及盡你最大的可能發揮靈性。”因為這是在初級星球上的必修課，也是每一個正常出生在初級星球上的人要經歷的課題[3]。

If you understand this principle, then you will understand what is said in the book "Thiaoouba Prophecy ": you are on your planet in order to learn how to live, suffer and die, but also to develop spiritually as much as you can." Because this is a compulsory course on a primary planet, and it is also a lesson that every normal person born on the primary planet must experience [3].

注 Note

[1] 每一個靈魂都擁有自由的意志，願意體驗二元世界的“哪一邊”，只能由自己的內心來決定。實際上，改變了自己的內心，就等於改變了自己的世界。

Every soul has a free will, which side of the "dual world" you are willing to experience can only be decided by your own heart. In fact, changing one's heart is equivalent to changing one's world.

[2] “地球是一個初級修煉場，隨著一個人的靈魂進化程度不斷地提升，在轉世時可以到一個更好的環境去體驗下一世的生活。”此知識點出自《海奧華預言》第六章。

"The earth is a primary training ground. As a person's soul evolves, he can go to a better environment to experience the next life when reincarnated. "This knowledge point comes from the sixth chapter of "Thiaoouba Prophecy".

[3] 正常出生在地球上的人類，本身就是要經歷一些 "課題" 來鍛煉自己的靈性。只不過目前的地球人把環境破壞得太嚴重，再加上人們不斷地追求 "物質主義、金錢主義"，把原本的 "課題" 變得更加扭曲、複雜和難解了。

Normally, humans born on Earth have to go through some "lessons" to exercise their spirituality. However, the current people on Earth have destroyed the environment too seriously, and coupled with people's constant pursuit of "materialism and money", the original "lessons" have become more distorted, complicated and difficult to solve.

附加文:
Additional text:

地球不是一個監獄
The earth is not a prison

有人說地球是一個"大染缸"也好，說地球是一個"監獄"也罷，但不管怎麼說，你目前轉到地球上的這一世，就一定是有原因的。要麼你有需要磨煉的內容，要麼你有某些任務在身。你之所以會成為現在的這個"你"，跟前些世犯過的錯和努過的力都有關。

Some people say that the Earth is like a "big dye vat", or they say it is a "prison". But no matter what you think, the fact is that the current life you have chosen to live on Earth must have a reason. Either you have something to work on for personal growth, or you have certain tasks to fulfill. The reason why you have become who you are now is related to the mistakes you made and the efforts you made in previous lives.

目前地球上的文明確實可以比作成一個"差生班"，可你是否想過，就算是再"差"的班，學校裡每階段也會選出能晉級的學生到"好的班級"。

The current civilization on Earth can indeed be compared to a "poor class", but have you ever thought that even in the "worst" class, the school will select students who can be promoted to the "good class" at each stage.

只要有學生儘量控制住，不學習某些"差生"的思想和行為，再更加自律一些，按照"教育局"（宇宙法則、自然法則）的規定去學習和生活，晉升到其他"優秀的班級"沒有問題。

As long as students try their best to control themselves, do not learn the thoughts and behaviors of certain "poor students", and be more self-disciplined, and study and live in accordance with the regulations of the "Education Bureau" (the laws of the universe, the laws of nature), there will be no problem in being promoted to other "excellent classes".

所以，目前在地球上的這一世，是選擇精進還是墮落，只能由你自己決定 [1]。

Therefore, in this life on Earth, whether you choose to progress or degenerate is up to you to decide [1].

注 Note

[1] 人的靈魂被賦予了絕對的自由意志，以至於人可以進化成像"聖賢"一樣的存在，也可以退化到像"食人族或野獸互相殘殺"那樣的存在，這在於一個人靈魂的自由選擇。

The human soul is endowed with absolute free will, so that humans can evolve into beings like "saints" or degenerate into beings like "cannibals or beasts killing each other", which depends on the free choice of your soul.

47

你的愛心程度決定著你"靈魂進化"的速度
The degree of your love determines the speed of your "soul evolution"

我們都知道，所有物質都是暫時為我們服務的工具，能獲得好的精神體驗才是最終目的。因為在輪回時，只有精神和靈魂會被我們帶走。

We all know that all material things are tools that serve us temporarily, and the ultimate goal is to gain a good spiritual experience, because in reincarnation, only the spirit and soul will be taken away by us.

"住在每個正常人體內的靈體，會將它在肉體裡的一生中所體驗到的所有感覺，傳遞給他的'高級自我'。"[1]

"The Astral body that resides in every normal human being transmits to his 'higher self' all the sensations he experiences during his lifetime in the physical body." [1]

通過這些信息我們就能大致地明白，我們每個靈魂在身體中的目的就是為了獲得體驗，同時體驗到的所有感覺也會通過大腦傳遞給自己的"高級自我"。那我們如何把這些體驗到的感覺，都儘量變成好的精神體驗，這才是最重要的。

Through this information, we can roughly understand that the purpose of each of our souls in the body is to gain experience, and all the feelings experienced will be transmitted to our "higher self" through the brain. So how can we try to turn these feelings into good spiritual experiences? This is the most important thing.

事實上，當一個人的內心充滿著愛 [2]，那麼他在遇到任何人或事物時，都能發現和體驗到"好"的一面。

In fact, when a person's heart is filled with love [2], he will be able to discover and experience the "good" side of anyone or anything he encounters.

可如果一個人的內心總帶有"恨"，那麼他在遇到任何人或事物時，都會感覺和體驗到種種的"不順眼"。

But if a person always carries "hatred" in his heart, then he will feel and experience all kinds of "displeasure" when he meets any person or thing.

並且，獲得"好與不好"的精神體驗，在絕大多數情況下，跟你能獲取到的"物質"也沒有太大的關係。

Moreover, in most cases, the spiritual experience of "good or bad" has little to do with the "material" things you can obtain.

舉個例子，桌子上有一把水果刀，你可以用它把水果切開，跟朋友們分享。你也可以拿這把水果刀，去超市做一個強盜，去威脅別人。

For example, there is a fruit knife on the table. You can use it to cut the fruit and share it with your friends. Or you can take this fruit knife and go to the supermarket to be a robber and threaten others.

也就是說，獲得"好與不好的"精神體驗，全在於你靈魂的自由意志。願意獲得"哪一邊"的感覺，也是由你當下的靈魂進化程度來決定的。

In other words, whether you get a "good or bad" spiritual experience depends entirely on the free will of your soul. The feeling of "which side" you are willing to get is also determined by the current level of your soul's evolution.

所以，在靈魂進化的道路上，先提高自己的"愛心程度"是一件非常重要的事情。也可以說，確實是"愛心程度"在決定著我們靈魂進化的速度。♡

Therefore, on the path of soul evolution, it is very important to first improve your "degree of love". It can also be said that it is indeed the "degree of love" that determines the speed of our soul evolution.♡

注 Note

[1] 人的一生，會把他從肉體中體驗到的所有感覺，傳遞給他的"高級自我"。
"這些感覺在到達圍繞著神靈的以太'海洋'前，需要通過由九個高級自我組成的巨大'濾網'。如果這些感覺本質上是基於物質主義的，高級自我們就會在過濾它時遇到巨大的麻煩，就像一個濾水網在過濾髒水時，會比過濾已經乾淨的水時更容易堵塞。通過人生中眾多的體驗，你確使自己的星光體在精神層面受益，它會學到越來越多的靈性知識。

隨著時間的推移，可能是地球上的 500 甚至 15000 年不等的時間，你的高我將沒什麼需要過濾的了。體現在星光體中的這部分高我將達到很高的精神境界，它將進入下一個階段。我們可以將這個過程看作一個九級過濾器，通過九個不同的濾網來過濾流經的水。當第一級過濾結束後，第一個濾網將完全消失，那麼就還剩下八個。當然，為了讓這些信息更容易理解，我用了大量的比喻…

因此，在完成和第一級高我的循環後，星光體將脫離一級高我，重新加入第二級高我；整個過程將會重複。

同樣，星光體也會因精神境界足夠高而轉世到下一個等級的星球上去。"此段文字出自《海奧華預言》第六章。（星光體就是我們所說的靈體、靈魂）

我們很多人都知道"人的靈魂會有轉世輪回"，但靈魂為什麼要轉世輪回是大多數人不知道的。

而這些信息就是我們轉世輪回的真實目的，因為我們每個靈魂都要在精神層面不斷地提升自己，要讓自己變得更加完美，最終才能回到我們偉大的源頭。

Your Astral body, which inhabits every normal human being, transfers to its Higher-self all the sensations that are experienced during a lifetime in a physical body.

"These sensations pass through the immense 'filter' of nine Higher-selves before arriving in the etheric 'ocean' that surrounds the Spirit. If these sensations are based essentially on materialism, the Higher-selves have enormous trouble filtering them, just as a water filter clogs quicker if it filters dirty water than if the water was already clear. 'If, through the numerous experiences you have in your life, you ensure your Astral body benefits in a spiritual sense, it will acquire more and more spiritual understanding.

In time, which can vary from 500 to even 15 000 of your Earth years, your Higher-self will have nothing more to filter. This part of itself, embodied in the Astral being of Michel Desmarquet, will be so spiritually advanced, it will have arrived at the next stage where it will have to contend directly with the more superior Higher-self. We can compare this process with a nine-stage filter, intended to rid the water passing through, of nine elements. At the end of stage one in the process, one will have been completely eliminated, with eight remaining. Of course, to make this information easier to digest, I am making enormous use of imagery...

This Astral body then, will have completed its cycle with the Higher-self of the first category and will then detach itself from Higher-self number one to rejoin the Higher-self of the second category; the entire process will be repeated.

By the same token, the Astral body will be sufficiently spiritually advanced to pass to a planet of the next category, as well. "This passage is from the sixth chapter of "Thiaoouba Prophecy".

Many of us know that "the human soul will reincarnate", but most people don't know why the soul will reincarnate.

And this information is the real purpose of our reincarnation, because each of our souls must constantly improve ourselves on the spiritual level, to make ourselves more perfect, and finally return to our Great Source.

[2] 假如生活中遇到了一件事情讓你左右不定的時候，請儘量要偏向有愛心的那一邊做決定。

當然，愛的裡面肯定包含著"寬容"和"包容"，可"寬容和包容"並不代表著可以去"縱容"，縱容一個正在犯錯的人或一件錯誤的事情，那不屬於愛的範疇。

而如何判斷你的做法是"包容"還是"縱容"，這就要發揮一個人靈性中的智慧了。

在某些程度上，如果你真心實意地想讓"某個人或某件事物"，在正確的道路上變得越來越好，這或許就是我們所說的真愛吧。

If you encounter something in life that makes you undecided, please try to make a decision with love in mind.

Of course, love definitely includes "tolerance and forgiveness", but "tolerance and forgiveness" does not mean that you can "indulge".

Indulging a person who is making a mistake or a wrong thing does not fall into the category of love.

As for how to judge whether your behavior is "tolerance" or "indulgence", this requires the wisdom of one's spirituality.

To some extent, if you sincerely want to make "someone or something" better and better on the right track, this may be what we call true love.

48

你可以擁有"天地人合一"的感覺，
也可以釋放出更多感知美好的能力
You can have the feeling of "unity of heaven,
earth and man", and you can also release
more abilities to perceive beauty.

"如果你問我這世界有沒有一個'造物者'，那我想是有的，因為整個世界的結構不是偶然的。你看我面前的麥克風，它也不是偶然的，偶然就不會出現這麼妙的東西。在我 20 歲左右的時候，對'造物者'這種說法是堅決反對的，可年齡漸漸大了以後，這個反對的動力在降低，發現這世界上妙的東西多得不得了……"這是楊振寧先生，在談造物主時說過的一段話。

"If you ask me if there is a "creator" in this world, I think there is, because the structure of the entire world is not accidental. Look at the microphone in front of me, it is not accidental either, such a wonderful thing would not appear by chance. When I was about 20 years old, I was firmly opposed to the idea of a "creator", but as I got older, the motivation to oppose it was reduced, and I found that there are so many wonderful things in this world... "This is a passage that Mr. Yang Chen-Ning said when talking about the creator.

這也是為什麼很多著名的科學家，到了晚年都開始相信"造物主"存在的原因。然而這宇宙中所有的一切：行星、恒星、植物、動物，也確實都是被造物主精心設計過的 [1]。

This is also why many famous scientists began to believe in the existence of the "Creator" in their later years. However, everything in the universe: planets, stars, plants, animals, are indeed carefully designed by the Creator [1].

一個人的精神境界越高，就越會喜歡接近大自然；而如果這個人知道了世界上所有的一切，都是被造物主精心設計過的，那麼他就算看到一片樹葉，也會從心裡感覺到這世界的精緻與美好。

The higher a person's spiritual level is, the more he will like to be close to nature; and if this person knows that everything in the world is carefully designed by the Creator, then even if he sees a leaf, he will feel the exquisiteness and beauty of the world from the bottom of his heart.

進一步講，如果這個人再知道了"人、動物、花草樹木"也都是"造物主"的化身 [2]，那麼自己在進入大自然時，就會很容易地和大自然融入一起。此時你將會體驗到那種"天、地、人合一"的親切感覺，這種感覺會非常非常的棒！

Furthermore, if this person knows that "people, animals, flowers, plants, and trees" are also incarnations of the "Creator" [2], then when he enters nature, he will be able to blend in with nature very easily. At this point, you will experience the intimate feeling of "the unity of heaven, earth, and man", and this feeling will be very, very good!

並且，擁有這些更高級的"美好感覺"，是因為你"感知美好能力”的提升而獲得的；而一個人的“感知美好能力”與一個人的“靈魂進化程度”[3]，又存在著直接的關係；

Furthermore, these higher-level "good feelings" are acquired through the improvement of your "ability to perceive good things"; and there is a direct relationship between a person's "ability to perceive good things" and their "degree of soul evolution" [3].

我們現在思考一個問題，一個人你看她是否美麗？或一朵花你是否能夠聞到香氣？這些基本的“感知美好能力”，從來就沒有人教過你，可你為什麼會感覺，這種長相的人就是美的？這種花散發的氣味就是香的？為什麼會有這些自發的美好感覺出現？

Let's think about a question now. Do you think a person is beautiful? Or can you smell the fragrance of a flower? These basic "abilities to perceive beauty" have never been taught by anyone, but why do you feel that a person with this appearance is beautiful? The smell of this flower is fragrant? Why do these spontaneous feelings of beauty appear?

也許原因就是，我們現有的這些基礎的“感知美好能力”，是造物主早就為我們提前釋放出來的。

Perhaps the reason is that these basic abilities we have now to "perceive beauty" were already released for us by the Creator long ago.

然而當我們的靈魂逐漸進化以後，我們就可以釋放出更多感知美好的能力。

However, as our souls gradually evolve, we can release more abilities to perceive beauty.

比如，你聽完了某首音樂，你的全身感覺非常舒服；讀完了某本書上的內容，你從心裡感覺到了滿足；幫助了某個人或動物，讓你感覺到了發自內心的喜悅；走進大自然時，又讓你感覺到了無比的親切，等等。

For example, after listening to a piece of music, your whole body feels very comfortable; after reading a book, you feel satisfied from the bottom of your heart; helping a person or an animal makes you feel happy from the bottom of your heart; when you walk into nature, you feel an overwhelming sense of closeness, and so on.

這些更高級的美好感覺，如果在以前你沒有感覺到，而現在卻感覺到了。這是因為你靈魂進化程度的提高，釋放出了更多感知美好的能力。也就是說，是你靈魂進化程度的提升，讓你擁有了比最初更多的"感知美好能力"。

If you didn't feel these higher-level beautiful feelings before, but now feel them, it's because your soul's level of evolution has increased, releasing more abilities to perceive beauty. In other words, it's the improvement of your soul's level of evolution that has given you more "abilities to perceive beauty" than you initially had.

而感知美好能力的提升，又可以讓我們獲得更多"好的精神體驗"，這些"好體驗"又可以進一步讓我們的靈魂得到進化。

The improvement of our ability to perceive beauty can enable us to have more "good spiritual experiences", and these "good experiences" can further evolve our souls.

就這樣，我們的"靈魂"在這三種"因素"的互相推動下，或許可以加速轉動著在輪回體系中向上進步，直至回到我們偉大的源頭——造物主的懷抱。

In this way, under the mutual promotion of these three "factors", our "soul" may be able to accelerate its rotation and progress upward in the reincarnation system until it returns to the embrace of our great source - the Creator.

[插图含义：壹個星光體（靈魂）在二元壹體的世界裏（那個背景的白色和黑色代表了二元壹體的世界），靈魂通過釋放自己的愛心，讓自己的靈魂進化程度變高，從而獲得更多感知美好的能力，又從而獲得更多好的精神體驗，這樣向上輪回的速度也會更快。

最上邊的那個紫粉色星系，代表了造物主的懷抱，同時代表了最高的智慧與愛，也代表了造物主在創造宇宙萬物時使用的 4 種宇宙力]

[Illustration meaning: An Astral body (soul) exists in a dualistic unity world (the white and black background in that picture represent the dualistic unity world). The soul evolves by releasing its love, thereby increasing its level of soul evolution and obtaining more abilities to perceive beauty, and thus experiencing more positive spiritual experiences. As a result, the upward cycle speed will also be faster.

The purple-pink galaxy at the top represents the Creator's embrace, as well as the highest wisdom and love, and also represents the four types of cosmic forces used by the Creator when creating all things in the universe.]

注 Note

[1] "太初一切皆無，除了黑暗和一個靈魂，那靈魂便是神靈。神靈（The Spirit、造物主），他用他那極大的力量創造了一切物理形式的存在。他創造了行星、恒星、植物、動物，為了一個目的：滿足祂的精神需要。這是十分合理的事情，因為他是一個純精神"。

神靈在創世之初，同時使用了四種超級力量，分別是：

一、原子力（Atomic force）：所有的世界、恒星和原子都形成了，行星開始繞著它們的太陽轉，可能還會有自己的衛星，等等。

二、卵宇宙力（Ovocosmic Force）：神靈通過第二種力，構思了許多原始的動植物及由此衍生出的亞種，這些動植物都是由各種簡單的宇宙射線變成的宇宙卵創造的。

三、卵星體力（Ovoastromic Force）：太初，神靈想通過一種特殊的生物來體驗感情。於是他通過第三種力想像出了人類，由此，人類誕生了。

四、靈性力（Spirituality Force）：創世者需要通過一個物質世界來尋找精神體驗，為了獲得這些體驗，他想讓他靈魂的一小部分在一個肉體中顯現。於是他把自己靈魂極微小的一部分"植入"了人體，構成了人類的靈體。

第四種力的作用十分重要：它將神靈所想像的一切都實現了。同時神靈也利用第四種力規定了行星的九個等級（九個類別），靈體最初需要先從第一級星球開始生存，通過人生中眾多的體驗和靈性上的鍛煉，它會使自己的精神層面獲得受益。當達到更高的精神境界時，靈體可以轉世到更高一級的星球，去體驗更高級的生活環境。靈體通過在生命輪回體系中一步步地提升進化（這種進化是指精神層面的進化，而非物質層面的），直至晉升到第九級星球。通過在 1 到 9 類星球上的進化，最終可以重返我們偉大的源頭——回到造物主的懷抱。

（文中的神靈、造物主、創世者為同一個意思，靈體和靈魂為同一個意思）

詳細內容請查閱《海奧華預言》第 4 章和第 6 章，解開奧秘的鑰匙就在其中。

"in the beginning there was the Spirit alone and he created, by his immense force, all that exists materially. He created the planets, the suns, plants, animals, with one goal in mind: to satisfy his spiritual need. This is quite logical since he is purely spirit.. "

At the beginning of creation, God(Creator) used four Universe Forces at the same time, namely:

1. Atomic force: All the worlds and stars and atoms were formed, planets began to orbit their suns, possibly with their own moons, and so on.

2. Ovocosmic Force: Through the second force, God conceived the primary living creatures and many of the primary plants, all of these creatures and plants were created by simple cosmic rays, which ended up with cosmic eggs.

3.Ovoastromic Force: At the very beginning, the Spirit imagined experiencing feelings through a special creature. He had imagined Man by means of the third force that we will call the 'Ovoastromic

Force'. Thus Man was created.

4.Spirituality Force: The Creator needed a material world for spiritual experiences, and in order to obtain these experiences, he wanted a small part of his soul to manifest in a physical body. So he "implanted" a tiny part of his soul into the human body, forming the human Astral body.

The Fourth force had a very important role to play: it had to bring to fruition all that The Spirit(Creator) had imagined. At the same time, the Creator also use the fourth force to define nine levels (nine categories) of planets. The Astral body must first survive on the first-level planet. Through many experiences and spiritual training in life, it will benefit its spiritual level. When reaching a higher spiritual realm, the Astral body can reincarnate to a higher-level planet to experience a higher-level living environment. The Astral body will gradually improve and evolve in the reincarnation system (this evolution refers to the spiritual level, not the material level) until it is promoted to the ninth-level planet. Through the evolution on planets from 1 to 9, we can eventually return to our great source - back to the embrace of the Creator.

(The Spirit, God and Creator in this text have the same meaning, and the Soul and Astral body have the same meaning)

For details, please refer to Chapters 4 and 6 of "Thiaoouba Prophecy", "the key to the mystery" is among them.

[2] 人的靈體（靈魂）是由大約 40 萬億億個電子組成，而在當世的物理生命剛結束的時候（也就是靈魂進行下一次轉世之前），其中 19％的電子會重新變為宇宙的電子，直到在自然的要求下形成一個新的人體、一棵新的樹或動物；而剩下的那 81％會和他的高級自我重新匯合。也就是說我們和植物、動物都同屬一個

巨大的生命網絡，都可以看成一個整體，都是造物主自己的一部分。而人類是一種靈性最高，且擁有神靈一絲神性的特殊生命體，體內擁有 9 個命體，而動物一般只有 3 個。詳細內容請查閱《海奧華預言》第 13 章。

The human Astral body (soul) is composed of about four billion trillion electrons. When the physical life in this world just ends (that is, before the soul goes to the next reincarnation), 19% of the electrons will become electrons of the universe again, until a new human body, a new tree or an animal is formed under the requirements of nature; and the remaining 81% will reunite with his higher self. In other words, we, plants and animals all belong to a huge life network, and can be regarded as a whole, and are all part of the Creator himself. Humans are a special life form with the highest spirituality and a trace of divinity. Humans have 9 bodies, while animals generally have only 3. For details, please refer to chapter 13 of the "Thiaoouba Prophecy".

[3] 如何檢測自己當下的靈魂進化程度是提高了還是下降了？你只需要真誠地觀察自己的興趣愛好即可，比如：如果你當下的靈魂進化程度降低了，那麼你在面對一些暴力、汙穢、奢靡、陰暗等一些負面的事情時，就會很感興趣。相反，如果你當下的靈魂進化程度變高了，那麼你就會對一些愛心、光明、優雅、平和等一些正面的事情，更感興趣。

然而這一切的興趣來源於獲得的信息與你當下的"靈魂進化程度"產生了某種共振。

How to detect whether your current soul evolution degree has increased or decreased? You only need to sincerely observe your own interests and hobbies. For example, if your current soul evolution level has decreased, you will be very interested in some negative things such as violence, filth, luxury, darkness, etc. On the contrary, if your current soul evolution level has increased, you will be more interested in some positive things such as love, brightness, elegance, peace, etc.

However, all this interest comes from the fact that the information obtained resonates with your current "degree of soul evolution".

49

因果業力真實存在，可"功過"為什麼不會相抵？
Karma really exists, but why don't "doing good things and doing bad things" cancel each other out?

"你向河中扔了一塊石頭，也許你轉身就能忘記了這件事情，可那塊石頭卻一直會在那河底躺著。"這就是大自然的記錄，是絕對真實無虛假的記錄。

"You throw a stone into the river. Maybe you will turn around and forget about it, but the stone will always lie at the bottom of the river." This is the record of nature, an absolutely true record without falsehood.

而"高級自我"的記錄[1]和"大自然的記錄"是同一個道理，同樣也是絕對真實無虛假的。

The records of the "Higher Self"[1] are the same as the "records of Nature" and are also absolutely true and without falsehood.

"轉世輪回"對每個靈魂來說確實是一個極其複雜的過程，但"高級自我"們作為純神靈的分支[2]，祂會厘清你做過的每一件事，然後將你的靈體匹配到合適的生活環境中。

Reincarnation is indeed an extremely complex process for every soul, but the Higher Selves, as branches of The Spirit [2], will clarify everything you have done and then match your soul to a suitable living environment.

也正因為"高級自我"真實無虛假地記錄著我們做過的每一件事，所以"因果業力"就會真實無虛假地在輪回體系中持續地運行著。

It is precisely because the "higher self" records everything we have done truthfully and without falsehood that the "karma" will continue to operate truthfully and without falsehood in the reincarnation system.

那麼"功過"自然也就不會"相抵"，而是"該獎的會獎，該罰的就會罰" [3]。

Then, "doing good things and doing bad things" will naturally not "cancel each other out", but rather "things that deserve to be rewarded will be rewarded, and things that deserve to be punished will be punished" [3].

簡單來說就是：你曾經幫助過多少人，未來的你就會獲得多少好運和幫助。你給別人創造過多少快樂，那麼你自己將來也會獲得多少快樂。

To put it simply: the more people you have helped, the more good luck and help you will get in the future. The more happiness you have created for others, the more happiness you will get in the future.

同樣，你曾經為難過多少人，未來的你就會受到多少為難。你給別人創造過多少痛苦，那麼你自己將來也會體驗到這些痛苦。

Likewise, the more people you have oppressed in the past, the more oppression you will suffer in the future. The more pain you have caused others, the more pain you will experience in the future.

要記住，一個人給別人創造的任何一種感覺，未來都會以不同的方式體驗到他自己身上。

Remember that any feeling a person creates for others will be experienced by himself in a different way in the future.

因為宇宙本身就是一個整體，我們每一個人都是造物主自己的化身。你傷害別人就等於傷害造物主，也等於傷害自己。同樣的道理，你關愛別人也等於關愛造物主，也等於關愛你自己。

Because the universe itself is a whole, each of us is the incarnation of the Creator himself. If you hurt others, you are hurting the Creator, and you are hurting yourself. In the same way, if you care about others, you are caring about the Creator, and you are caring about yourself.

如果懂得了以上這些道理，那麼你就會明白：

If you understand the above principles, then you will understand:

你的福報，都是因為你累世做過的事情而得來的。

Your blessings are all due to the things you did in your past lives.

你的業報，也都是因為你累世做過的事情而得來的 [4]。

Your karmic retribution is also the result of the things you did in your past lives. [4]

所以，我們每個人都需要明白，做一個正直善良有愛心的人，並不全是為了別人，而更多的是為了我們"未來的自己"。

Therefore, each of us needs to understand that being an honest, kind and loving person is not entirely for others, but more for our "future self".

為了今生和來世的自己，請做一個正直善良有愛心的人吧，因為我們每個靈魂的目標，都是要在輪回的終點獲得"永恆的幸福"。

For the sake of your own life in this life and the next, please be an honest, kind and loving person, because the goal of each of our souls is to obtain "eternal happiness" at the end of reincarnation.

[1] 每個人都有自己的"高級自我"，高級自我會記錄著我們做過的每一件事情。而且"高我"不止記錄著我們的一言一行，我們體驗到的所有感覺也會通過大腦傳遞給自己的"高我"。仔細想想我們的頭髮為什麼基本向上生長？而且頭頂的發旋和星系的模樣基本相似，這或許也有著一定的原因吧。

Everyone has their own "higher self", which records everything we do. Moreover, the "higher self" not only records our every word and deed, but also all the feelings we experience are transmitted to our "higher self" through the brain. Think about it, why do our hairs basically grow upwards? And the spiral at the top of our head is basically similar to the shape of a galaxy. Maybe there is a certain reason for this as well.

[2] "宇宙的模式決定了九顆行星繞著它們的恒星轉。同樣，這些恒星也在繞著更大的恒星轉，這更大的恒星就是九個這樣的恒星及其行星的核心。這樣繼續下去，一直追溯到宇宙的中心。"（我們的靈魂在輪回體系中的進化模式，和行星恒星在星系中的運行模式非常相似，因為都是造物主設計創造的）

"神靈（造物主）利用第四種力，把自己靈魂極微小的一部分'植入'了人體，構成了人類的靈體。靈體是一個人體必要的九分之一，其中包括了'高級自我'，有時也被稱為'超我'。

"換句話說，人的高級自我是一個實體，它把自己的九分之一潛入一個人的身體中，成為人的靈體，其餘肉體也被同一個高級自我的其餘九分之一居住，不過每部分對中央實體來說都是不可或缺的。（也就是說，在地球上我們每個人都有另外 8 個'同一高我'的兄弟姐妹）

"進一步講，一個一級高我是一個二級高我的九分之一；相應地，這個二級高我也是一個三級高我的九分之一。這個過程繼續下去，直到本源，神靈需要的精神體驗便由此經過了巨大的過濾。"

此段文字出自《海奧華預言》第六章，書內有詳細描述。

[2] "The pattern of the Universe dictates that nine planets revolve around their sun. It is also the case that these suns revolve around a bigger sun, which is the nucleus for nine such suns, and their nine planets. So it continues, right to the centre of the Universe from where the explosion referred to by the English as the 'Big Bang' originated." (The evolutionary pattern of our souls in the reincarnation system is very similar to the pattern of planets and stars in the galaxy, because they are all designed and created by the Creator.)

"The Spirit (the Creator) uses the fourth force to 'inserted' an infinitesimal part of his soul into the human body, forming the human Astral body. The Astral body is the necessary ninth part of a human body, which includes the 'higher self', sometimes also called the 'overself'.

"The Higher-self of man is, in other words, an entity which sends one ninth of itself into a human body, becoming the person's Astral being.

Other physical bodies are inhabited, similarly, by other ninths of the same Higher-self and yet each part remains integral to the central entity. (That is to say, on the earth, each of us has eight other brothers and sisters with the same higher self.)

"Further, the Higher-self is a ninth part of a superior Higher-self which, in turn, is a ninth part of a more superior Higher-self. The process continues as far back as the source, and allows the enormous filtration of spiritual experience required by the Spirit."

This passage is from the sixth chapter of "Thiaoouba Prophecy", which is described in detail.

[3] "宇宙法則是完善的，它就像恆星控製著行星轉動一樣嚴格的運作著，如果你犯了一個錯誤，你就會受到懲罰——可能是立刻，可能是十年後或是十個世紀後，但不管多久，你都必須為自己的錯誤付出代價。"此段文字出自《海奧華預言》第三章。

"Universal Law is well-established and is as strictly enforced as that which controls the planets revolutions around their suns. If you make a mistake, you pay the penalty - immediately, in ten years time, or in ten centuries time, but errors must be paid for "This passage is from the third chapter of "Thiaoouba Prophecy".

[4] 這裡的"福報"並不是單指物質上的富足，而是你內心裡能夠獲得的那種幸福、喜悅和其他的一些美好感覺。而"業報"也不是單指生活中遇到的困難，更多的是你曾經給別人帶來的某些不好的感覺，這些感覺也會在未來的時間裡讓你自己嘗試。

The "blessings" here do not refer only to material wealth, but to the happiness, joy and other good feelings you can get in your heart. And the "karmic retribution "does not refer only to the difficulties encountered in life, but more to some bad feelings you have brought to others, which will also make you experience them in the future.

要記住：我們每個人都擁有造物主的一絲神性，每個人的內在都擁有著偉大的精神力量，每一個人都是本自具足。你能創造多少愛給這個 "世界"，這個世界就會讓你擁有多少愛的感覺。也許是本世，也許是下一世，但不管多久，你創造出來的感覺，都會在未來的某個時間裡回饋給你自己。

Remember: Each of us has a trace of the Creator's divinity, each of us has great spiritual power within us, and everyone is inherently complete. How much love you can create for this "world" is how much love this world will give you. Maybe it will be in this life, maybe in the next life, but no matter how long it takes, the feelings you create will be returned to you at some time in the future.

愛永遠是宇宙中最偉大的力量

Love is always the greatest force in the universe.

50

種下"命運的種子"，收穫"永恆的幸福"
Plant the "seeds of destiny" and reap "eternal happiness"

很多人困惑於為什麼轉世前，靈體（靈魂）能夠簡單預覽自己的下一世？為什麼是自己選擇的自己的這一生？

Many people are confused as to why the soul can simply browse its next life before reincarnation? Why is it that one chooses one's own life?

其實你可以這樣理解，也許不全是因為你的靈體轉世到了這個地方，這個地方才出現了"這樣的一個人"。而是因為"*********"[1]，"這樣的一個人"即將可以在某個時間地點出現了，而你的靈體恰好能夠匹配這個"角色"，所以你才選擇轉世到了這裡，這個地方才出現了"這樣的一個人"。

In fact, you can understand it this way: maybe it's not entirely because your soul reincarnated to this place that "such a person" appeared here. Rather, it is because "*********" [1], "such a person" is about to appear at a certain time and place, and your Astral body happens to match this "role", so you choose to reincarnate here, and "such a person" appears in this place.

　　來到這一世，除了能讓自己學到一部分"新知識"以外，也可以讓自己還掉一部分前些世產生的"業力"。當然，在新命運的"課題"中，一般也會有新的"困難"來對你進行考驗（有時也會有一些誘惑的考驗）。而這些命運中的"課題"，也都是在你轉世前就已經從"高我"那裡簡單地預覽過了，因為你感覺自己能夠克服這些"課題"，能讓自己的靈魂學到更多、能使自己的靈性變得更高，所以才選擇了這一世的"人生劇本"。

In this life, in addition to learning some "new knowledge", you can also pay off some of the "karma" from previous lives. Of course, in the "lessons" of your new destiny, there will generally be new "difficulties" to test you (sometimes there will also be some temptations). And these "lessons" in destiny have all been briefly reviewed by your "higher self" before you reincarnated. Because you feel that you can overcome these "lessons", which can make your soul learn more and make your spirituality higher, you chose the "life script" of this life.

　　你自告奮勇地轉世到了現在這個地方，也一定是感覺自己能夠勝任這個"角色"。

You volunteered to reincarnate into your current place, and you must have felt that you were capable of fulfilling this "role".

　　如果這一世你經得起這些考驗，那麼你這一世就可以得到你想要的果報。而如果這一世你沒有經得起某些考驗，那麼在輪回時，就會帶著本世學到的"一些知識"（也會有"一些後悔"[2]），去選擇下一世的"課題"。

If you can overcome these tests in this life, then you will receive the results you desire in this life. If you do not overcome certain tests in this life, then when you reincarnate, you will take with you the "knowledge" you have learned in this life (and also "regrets" [2]) to choose the "lessons" for your next life.

所以，能不能"演好"自己選擇的"人生劇本"，就要看你自己這一世靈性的發揮了 [3]。

Therefore, whether you can "perform well" the "life script" of your own choice depends on your own spiritual development in this life [3].

那為什麼說，人可以為自己種下"命運的種子"？

Then why is it said that people can plant the "seeds of destiny" for themselves?

這裡首先我們需要看一下這個例子：

Here we need to look at this example first:

假如我們現在開始往籃球筐裡投籃，籃球離手出現拋物線到達籃筐的用時需要 1 秒鐘，而我們在這 1 秒鐘之後，才能知道籃球到底會不會進入到籃筐裡。

If we start shooting into the basket now, it will take 1 second for the basketball to leave our hand and form a parabola to reach the basket. Only after this 1 second can we know whether the basketball will enter the basket.

而事實卻是在你的手對球發"力"的瞬間，這顆籃球就已經被註定了走向（或命運），雖然籃球到達籃筐的時間用了一秒鐘，但這一秒鐘只是籃球命運過程中的一個顯象，而它到底能不能進入到籃筐裡，卻全在於你手最初發出的這個"力"。

But the fact is that the moment your hand exerts "force" on the ball, the trajectory (or destiny) of the basketball has already been determined. Although it takes one second for the basketball to reach the basket, this second is only a manifestation of the basketball's destiny process. Whether it can enter the basket depends entirely on the "force" initially exerted by your hand.

也就是說這個"力"就可以看作是這件事情的"因"，雖然用了1秒鐘之後才能知道球有沒有進入到籃筐裡，但投籃者的手在發"力"的瞬間，就已經決定了這件事情的"果"。

In other words, this "force" can be regarded as the "cause" of this event. Although it takes one second to know whether the ball has entered the basket, the shooter's hand has already determined the "result" of this event at the moment the "force" is exerted.

同樣，我們每個人都在不斷地種下"因"的種子，其實"種子"就等於你最初發出的一種"力"，而這股"力"在發出的瞬間，宇宙中就已經會有某種"結果"被瞬間感應到，只是等待某種時機的到來，再將"果"給你呈現出來。

Similarly, each of us is constantly sowing the seeds of "cause". In fact, the "seed" is equal to a kind of "force" that you initially emitted. The moment this "force" is emitted, some kind of "result" will be instantly sensed in the universe, just waiting for a certain opportunity to come before presenting the "result" to you.

事實上我們的每一個想法、每一個行動都可以看成一顆"因"的種子，這些"種子"如果在沒有被幹預的情況下會自然地生長，未來會長成什麼樣的形狀（軌跡），結出什麼樣的"果實"，基本已經註定。

In fact, every thought and every action we have can be seen as a seed of "cause". If these "seeds" are not interfered with, they will grow naturally. What shape (trajectory) they will grow into in the future and what kind of "fruit" they will bear are basically determined.

也就是說，是你原來種下的"因"，才收穫了現在生活中眾多出現的"果"。同樣，你本世的所作所為，也正在規劃著自己下一世要經歷的基本命運。

In other words, it is the "cause" you planted that has led to the many "results" that appear in your life now. Similarly, what you do in this life is also planning the basic destiny you will experience in the next life.

如果你懂得了這些道理，那麼就請為自己多種下愛心、友善、光明和那些正面的種子吧，你要相信自己，這些正面的種子一定會在你未來的生命中，為自己收穫到"永恆的幸福"。

If you understand these truths, then please plant more seeds of love, kindness, light and other positive things for yourself. You must believe in yourself that these positive seeds will definitely bring you "eternal happiness" in your future life.

注 Note

[1] 此處省略的內容已不被允許寫出，需讀者自行領悟。

The content omitted here is not allowed to be written out, and readers are required to understand it on their own.

[2] 命運的"課題"雖然是自己選擇好的，但很多人在填寫"課題的答案"時，有可能會"填錯"。靈魂在肉體中過完本世的生活時（就是在進行下一次轉世之前），都需要回溯自己這一生都做了

些什麼，而在靈體看著自己這一生回溯的"電影"時，有時會發現自己做錯了某些事情而感到後悔。

Although the "question" of fate is chosen by oneself, many people may "fill in the wrong answer" when filling in the "answer to the question". When the soul finishes its life in the flesh (that is, before the next reincarnation), it needs to look back on what it has done in this life. When the soul watches the "movie" of its life, it sometimes finds that it has done something wrong and feels regretful.

[3] 命運雖然大致安排了一些課題，但並不是說命運就不可以改，你可以往好的方向改，也可以往壞的方向改。如果這一世的自己頹廢墮落了，那麼有些"制定好的課題"也許這輩子根本不會碰到。而如果你通過自律進步了自己，那麼這一世就會"超額完成"一些從未學到的知識，靈魂進化程度就會獲得很高的提升，因為你擁有自由的意志。

還有些人一直困惑為什麼每個人大致的命運都是提前安排好的。

舉個例子：正常出生在初級星球的靈體，都可以比作成一到十幾歲的孩子，這個年齡段的孩子們需要上什麼學校，報什麼輔導班，去什麼遊樂場，大部分都是在"家長"的安排下才能完成的，而至於孩子們能不能"學好、玩開心"，全在於每個孩子靈性的自由發揮了，但"家長"們會看著這些孩子，不會過多地幹預。

而且就像在小學班級裡的學生那樣，學生們每天也必須有老師佈置好的一部分"作業"，這樣才能讓每個學生學到該學習的知識。而如果一開始就讓這些小學年級裡的小學生們都去自學，那麼他們肯定也不會知道該從何學起。

所以，我們每個人的靈魂都是在不斷地學習中，都需要不斷提升自己的精神層面，讓自己的靈魂進化程度更高，最終才能到達輪回的終點，重返我們偉大的源頭。

這裡的"家長"和"老師"都是指你的"高級自我"。

最後，要引用《海奧華預言》書中非常重要的一段話："一個靈性生命，在任何情況下，都必須遵循宇宙法則。並且，通過盡可能地順隨自然，他能夠以最快的途徑到達終極目標。"

愛，就是宇宙的基本法則。

終極目標，就是回到我們偉大的源頭，獲得永恆的幸福。

茫茫宇宙中，既然我們有緣能在同一個星球上"鍛煉和學習"，那麼就讓我們在未來的生命中，彼此關愛，共同進步吧！

Although fate has roughly arranged some lessons, it does not mean that fate cannot be changed. You can change it for the better or for the worse. If you are decadent in this life, then some of the "prepared lessons "may not be encountered in this life. If you improve yourself through self-discipline, then in this life you will "over-complete" some knowledge that you have never learned, and the degree of soul evolution will be greatly improved because you have free will.

Some people have always been confused about why everyone's general fate is arranged in advance.

For example: Souls born normally on the first type of planet can be compared to children from one to adolescence. What schools children of this age need to go to, what tutoring classes they need to sign up for, and what playgrounds they need to go to are mostly arranged by their "parents". As for whether the children can "learn well and have fun", it all depends on the free development of each child's spiritual potential, but the "parents" will watch these children and will not interfere too much.

And just like students in elementary school, students must have a portion of "homework" assigned by the teacher every day, so that each student can learn the knowledge they should learn. If these elementary school students are asked to study on their own from the beginning, they will definitely not know where to start.

Therefore, the soul of each of us is constantly learning, and we need to constantly improve our spiritual level and evolve our soul to a higher level, so that we can finally reach the end of reincarnation and return to our great source.

The "parent" and "teacher" here refer to your "higher self".

Finally, we should quote a very important passage in the book "Thiaoouba Prophecy": "An Astral body, in all cases, must conform to Universal Law, and, by following nature as closely as possible, it can achieve the ultimate goal by the fastest path."

Love is the basic law of the universe.

The ultimate goal is to return to our great source and obtain eternal happiness.

In the vast universe, since we are destined to "exercise and learn" on the same planet, let's care for each other and make progress together in our future lives!